Automotive Math Handbook

Forbes Aird

MOTORBOOKS
INTERNATIONAL

First published in 2000 by Motorbooks International, an imprint of MBI Publishing Company, Galtier Plaza, Suite 200, 380 Jackson Street, St. Paul, MN 55101-3885 USA

Motorbooks International titles are also available at discounts in bulk quantity for industrial or sales-promotional use. For details write to Special Sales Manager at Motorbooks International Wholesalers & Distributors, Galtier Plaza, Suite 200, 380 Jackson Street, St. Paul, MN 55101-3885 USA.

ISBN 0-7603-0696-6

On the front cover: From the speedways of NASCAR to the shade tree in the back yard, every mechanic relies on math. From cornering ability to horsepower, there are standardized formulas that a mechanic needs to know in order to determine proper tolerances, limits, and abilities of every aspect of an automobile. *Bill Burt*

On the back cover:
A task as simple as setting a car's timing relies on math. A timing light takes the guesswork out of the process, but to truly understand what the light is measuring, a few simple formulas come into play. A shade tree mechanic's next step beyond understanding the mechanism, is understanding the math that makes it work.

Edited by John Adams-Graf

Printed in the United States of America

Contents

Introduction

M y qualifications for writing this book are few, but convincing: I don't like math, never did, and am not very good at it. I fumbled through high-school math with grades that hovered around a "C," and in college just barely squeaked through first year calculus. I utterly bombed out of linear algebra. So, to say that I don't have a lot of what is called "natural aptitude" for mathematics would be to put it mildly.

So, where do I get off posing as the author of a book on the subject? Well, it's like this: I always wanted to be a race car designer, so I learned math the hard way—I taught myself.

After graduating from college (in English, I hasten to add), I worked at assorted boring desk jobs, but continued to hang around with the racers at the shop where I had worked after school for years, and so got involved in various race car projects. From these experiences, from looking and thinking, and from reading everything that I could get my hands on, I gradually learned more about engineering and mechanics and technology in general.

Among other things that I learned, it turns out that many of the *great* designers—Harry Miller, Ettore Bugatti, Frank Kurtis, Henry Royce, Henry Leland, Fred Offenhauser, Fred and Augie Duesenberg, Ferdinand Porsche— were about as inept at math as myself. This was a great consolation!

Alas, consolation was not enough. At one point, I accepted a consulting gig from a couple of guys who formed a company to produce a new type of race car brake. Now that I was actually being *paid*, in effect, to design race car stuff, I had to either fish or cut bait, as a matter of personal and professional pride. So I fished. Oh, I got a lot of hooks stuck in my fingers, and a lot of worm yuck on me, and I spent a lot of time with my line in the water with nary a nibble, but I gradually came to grips with math at a level that I could *use* in design calculations. I went back through all the books, engineering papers, and magazine clippings I had collected and painfully wrestled my way through every equation I thought I might ever need, and entered them all in a "little black book." Every time I encountered a new one, it went in the little black book.

I developed something of a reputation on the strength of that little black book; people often wondered what was in it. The answer is: chapters 2 through 7 of the book you have just bought. And thanks for buying it!

So, am I now the professional race car designer I always wanted to be? Nope, but I'm getting by, writing books about the subject ("Those who can, do; those who can't, teach." And I suppose those who can't teach, write!), still getting occasional consulting gigs . . . and I bet I am better at "motorhead math" than Harry Miller, Ettore Bugatti, Frank Kurtis. . . .

In my initial conversations about this book with my editor at MBI Publishing Company—then Zack Miller—the question arose as to the amount of explanation in terms of physics that would be needed to describe where the math itself should be applied. The upshot is that I have made an attempt to not simply present a series of equations but to explain what those equations mean, in words. That has led to a book with a lot of words. I have always found that if I can express a physical situation in words, then I can usually translate those words into a mathematical expression. And I am always leery and mistrustful when I encounter a *real* engineer (unlike myself) who offers blithe assurances that "the math works; don't worry about it," yet who cannot explain the *meaning* of a certain equation. Physical understanding comes first, in my view. I hope you find this approach useful.

Although it was Zack Miller's belief that it was reasonable to assume that potential readers would have a rudimentary knowledge of algebra, I decided to provide a brief review of that subject and some other basics in the first chapter, reasonably enough titled "Basics." If you can add, subtract, multiply, and divide, and if you work at it, you should be able to understand everything here. There's no calculus, and certainly no linear algebra! I should hasten to add that some of the equations here are very much simplified; to avoid boring you stupid, many secondary factors have been left out.

I am grateful to Zack (who has since been kicked upstairs to become publishing director at MBI Publishing Company) for offering me the contract for this book, and I wish also to thank John Adams-Graf, who took over as my editor, for his support and laid-back tolerance when, as seems always to happen to me, I became freaked out by the project.

I must explain that I did not personally *invent* any of the equations found here; they come from a great many sources, few of which I ever annotated in that little black book. Two that appear here, however, deserve acknowledgment: Thanks to Bill Ball of General Motors Canada who, together with a couple of colleagues, blew an hour or two of the General's time to come up with the equation on page 74 for me (my brain jammed up on this one!). I am also indebted to John Carlson of ADDCO Industries for the equation on page 79.

Thanks to reader Gila Eban for pointing out some errors and ommissions in the first print of the book.

Chapter 1

The Basics

Fractions, Decimals, and Percentages

The mathematical meaning of the term *fraction* is really no different from its general use: a portion or section, a piece of some whole thing. Fractions come in basically two kinds—simple fractions and decimal fractions.

A simple fraction is, in a sense, a "picture" of a division. It consists of two numbers, one above the other, separated by a horizontal line, or dash. The number above the line, called the *numerator*, is the number being divided, while the number below the line, the *denominator*, is the number doing the dividing. Thus, while $\frac{1}{3}$ is certainly "one-third," it equally certainly means "one divided by three." In what are called *proper fractions*, such as $\frac{1}{3}$, $\frac{3}{4}$, $\frac{5}{8}$ and so on, the numerator is smaller than the denominator, and thus the value of the fraction is always less than 1. In *improper fractions*, such as $\frac{8}{5}$, $\frac{7}{3}$, or $\frac{5}{2}$, the numerator is larger than the denominator, so the value is always more than 1. An improper fraction can be converted into what is called a *mixed number*—a combination of a whole number and a proper fraction—by carrying out the division that the fraction suggests, and leaving the remainder as a proper fraction. Thus, to convert $\frac{8}{5}$ into a mixed number, you simply divide 8 by 5. 5 goes into 8 once, with 3 left over, so $\frac{8}{5}$ is $1\frac{3}{5}$. In the same way, $\frac{7}{3}$ is $2\frac{1}{3}$, and $\frac{5}{2}$ is $2\frac{1}{2}$. There usually isn't a heck of a lot of point in performing this conversion from an improper fraction to a mixed number, but there are many situations where it is an advantage to perform the conversion the other way around—that is, converting a mixed number into an improper fraction. For instance, anytime you want to multiply together two mixed numbers, or a mixed number by a fraction, whether proper or improper, it is a lot easier if you turn the mixed number(s) into one or more improper fractions.

Multiplying and Dividing Simple Fractions

Perhaps surprisingly, multiplying two (or more) fractions together is generally a simpler matter than adding them. To multiply two fractions, you multiply the numerators together, then multiply the denominators. (Actually, it doesn't matter which you do first.) Consider, for example, $\frac{2}{3} \times \frac{3}{4}$. Dealing first with the numerators, $2 \times 3 = 6$, so the numerator in the result will be 6. As for the denominators, $3 \times 4 = 12$, so the denominator is 12, and the entire answer is $\frac{6}{12}$.

Most readers will surely recognize that $\frac{6}{12}$ is the same thing as $\frac{1}{2}$. If you don't, recall that we said above that a fraction is a division. If you divide 6 things (say pizzas) into 12 parts, the size of each resulting portion (that is, each *fraction*) is exactly the same as if you divided 1 pizza into 2 parts—half a pizza. Note that the way to get from $\frac{6}{12}$ to $\frac{1}{2}$ is to divide *both* the numerator *and* the denominator by 6. We can generalize from this to say that the value of a fraction remains the same if we divide the numerator and the denominator by the same number. Thus, $\frac{4}{8}$ is $\frac{1}{2}$ (divide both by 4), and so is $\frac{3}{6}$ (divide by 3) and $\frac{5}{10}$, and so on. Another way to think about the same thing is to divide both the numerator and the denominator by the numerator. Whenever you wind up with a fraction where the numerator will divide evenly into the denominator, or where both numerator and denominator are evenly divisible by the same whole number, you have the opportunity to *simplify* the fraction in this way—and you should.

Dividing fractions is a difficult concept to grasp (I personally have a hard time wrapping my head around this idea), but is just about as easy to do as multiplying them; there is just one extra step. To divide one fraction by

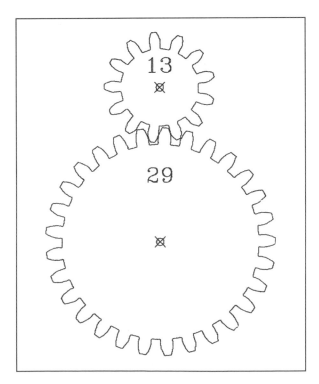

Figure 1
A ratio is not just something to do with gears; it is a mathematical relationship and is essentially the same thing as a fraction. In this case the ratio is 29:13, or 2.23:1 (29 divided by 13).

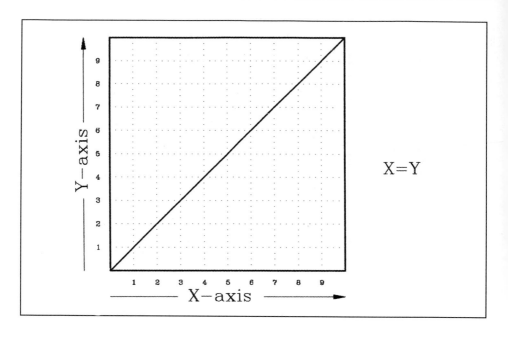

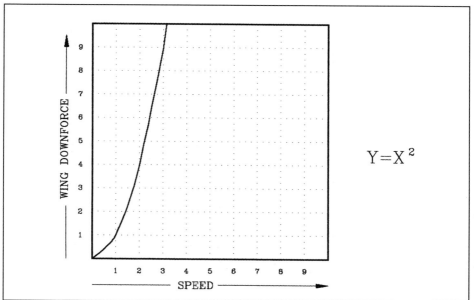

When graphed, exponents reveal the "shape" of a mathematical relationship. A linear relation (*Figure 2*, top left) produces a straight line; a "square law" relation (*Figure 3*, bottom left) involves a rapid rise of one value as the other increases linearly—a doubling of the one is associated with a fourfold increase of the other; in a "cubic"

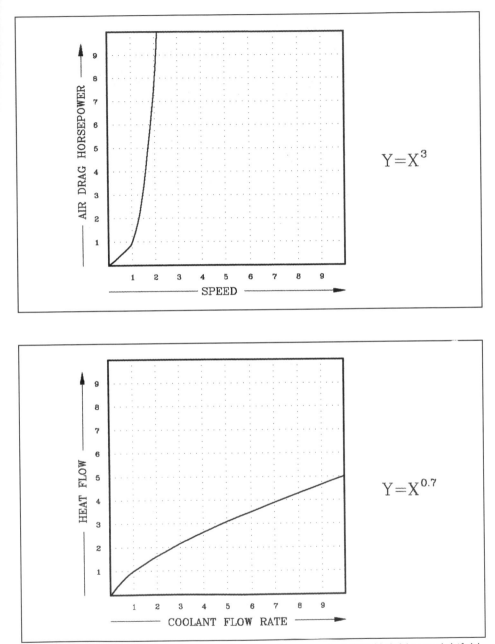

$$Y=X^3$$

$$Y=X^{0.7}$$

relation (*Figure 4,* top right), the curve is even steeper—doubling *X* yields an eightfold increase in *Y*; fractional exponents (*Figure 5,* bottom right) are characterized by a curve that tends to "flatten out."

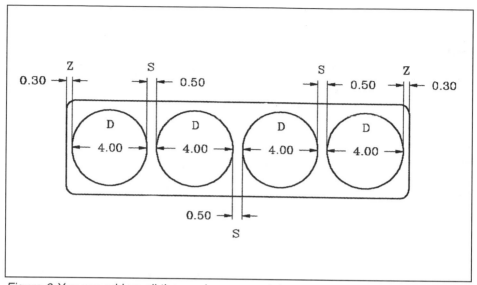

Figure 6: You can add up all the numbers separately, or you can group numbers that are the same and multiply.

another, first invert the numerator and denominator of the fraction following the "÷" sign, then multiply them together just as above. Let's take for an example $\frac{2}{3} \div \frac{3}{4}$. First invert the $\frac{3}{4}$ to make it $\frac{4}{3}$, then multiply $\frac{2}{3} \times \frac{4}{3}$. Multiplying the numerators, 2×4 equals 8, and multiplying the denominators, 3×3 equals 9, so the end result is $\frac{8}{9}$. (By the way, the horizontal line separating the numerator and denominator is called the *vinculum*. Now there is a word you can win some bar bets with!)

Adding and Subtracting Simple Fractions

Adding or subtracting fractions requires first finding what is called a *common denominator*. Perhaps the easiest way to describe this is by example. Suppose we want to add $\frac{2}{3}$ and $\frac{3}{4}$. Recall that we said above that "the value of a fraction remains the same if we divide the numerator and the denominator by the same number. Thus, $\frac{4}{8}$ is $\frac{1}{2}$ . . ." Well, if $\frac{4}{8} = \frac{1}{2}$, then $\frac{1}{2} = \frac{4}{8}$. So, if we can *divide* both the numerator and denominator of a fraction by the same number without changing the value of the fraction, then it must also be legitimate to *multiply* the numerator and denominator by the same number. OK, so let's multiply the numerator and denominator of $\frac{2}{3}$ by 4. That gives us $\frac{8}{12}$. Now let's multiply the numerator and denominator of $\frac{3}{4}$ by 3, which gives us $\frac{9}{12}$. Note that both the fractions we are trying to add, $\frac{8}{12}$ and $\frac{9}{12}$, now have the same denominator, 12. Now you simply add together the numerators: $8 + 9 = 17$. Thus,

$$\frac{2}{3} + \frac{3}{4} = \frac{8}{12} + \frac{9}{12} = \frac{17}{12}$$
(And, for what it is worth, $\frac{17}{12} = 1\frac{5}{12}$.)

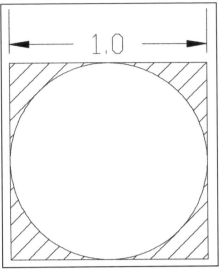

Figure 7: A 1-inch-diameter circle does *not* have an area of 1 square inch.

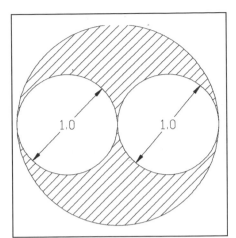

Figure 8: Just so there is no misunderstanding, the total area of two circles, each of 1-inch diameter, does *not* equal the area of a 2-inch diameter circle. Doubling the diameter yields four times the area.

It turns out that in the above example we wound up multiplying the first fraction by the denominator of the second one, and vice versa. This technique guarantees that we will arrive at a common denominator, but it may not be the *lowest* common denominator. Thus, for example, if we want to add $\frac{1}{6} + \frac{2}{3}$ we could proceed as above and get $\frac{3}{18} + \frac{12}{18} = \frac{15}{18}$. Then we could simplify $\frac{15}{18}$ by dividing both the numerator and denominator by 3 to get $\frac{5}{6}$. But we could just as easily multiply the $\frac{2}{3}$ by 2 to get $\frac{4}{6}$ (which has the denominator 6 in common with $\frac{1}{6}$), then add $\frac{1}{6} + \frac{4}{6} = \frac{5}{6}$.

You will always get a final answer with the correct value if you do this "cross multiplication" of denominators, but sometimes you wind up with an awkwardly large number for the common denominator, which makes the arithmetic tougher. If you immediately see that both of the numerators and the common denominator are divisible by the same whole number, then it is usually helpful to do so.

Subtracting fractions follows exactly the same procedure: first establish a common denominator, then subtract the one numerator from the other and, if appropriate, simplify the resulting fraction. For example:

$$\frac{5}{6} - \frac{3}{4} = \frac{20}{24} - \frac{18}{24} = \frac{2}{24} = \frac{1}{12} \text{ (using "cross multiplication")}$$

or:

$$\frac{5}{6} - \frac{3}{4} = \frac{10}{12} - \frac{9}{12} = \frac{1}{12} \text{ (both 6 and 4 divide evenly into 12)}$$

Ratios

Simple fractions can also be thought of as *ratios*, and vice versa. Thus, the ratio of 2:3 ("two-to-three") can be represented as $\frac{2}{3}$. Often when we speak of a "ratio" we are thinking about a gear ratio. Exactly the same notion of a fraction applies there, too. For instance, a gear with 13 teeth engaged with a gear having 29 teeth will have a ratio of 13:29, which can also be expressed as $\frac{13}{29}$ (or $\frac{29}{13}$, a gear ratio—for that matter any ratio—can be looked at "from either end." The ratio between the little gear and the big one is 13:29; the ratio between the big one and the little one is 29:13).

While the above is perfectly correct (and some folks *do,* in fact, express gear ratios this way), usually when a gear ratio is expressed it is a number with a decimal place, followed by ":1", like 2.23:1. In reality, "2.23:1" and "$\frac{29}{13}$" are exactly the same thing, just expressed differently. We have, in effect, divided both numerator and denominator by 13, thus producing a fraction with a denominator of 1 and a numerator that is a *decimal fraction*, as we shall now see.

Decimal Fractions

We encounter simple fractions often enough, particularly in the building trades, but decimal fractions crop up rather more often in automotive work. A lot of folks have problems with decimals, and especially in converting between the one type of fraction and the other, but there really is nothing complicated or difficult about decimals. They are simply fractions in which the denominator is always some multiple of 10 (i.e., 10, 100, 1,000, etc.) and is not explicitly written down. Instead, it is implied by the *location* of the number representing the numerator.

This may seem confusing at first (I apologize for the clumsy description above!), but it is really no different from the way we write large whole numbers. Thus, when we see 1,746 we all understand that there is 1 "thousand," 7 "hundreds," 4 "tens," and 6 "ones." If you were counting this number

Figure 9: The area of a rectangle is simply the length times the width.

of dollars out in bills and you wanted to use the smallest possible number of bills (and had no fins, only ones, sawbucks, hundreds, and thousands), those are exactly the numbers of respective bills you would count out.

Same thing with decimals. When you see "9.3125" the number is telling you that there are 9 "ones," 3 "tenths," 1 "hundredth," 2 "thousandths," and 5 "ten-thousandths." That's all there is to it. (The "." between the 9 and the 3 is called the *decimal point*, and the whole number would be read as "nine point three one two five," but then, you probably knew that.) So, 0.3 is exactly the same thing as $\frac{3}{10}$, 7.41 is exactly the same thing as $7\frac{41}{100}$, and 27.456 is exactly the same thing as $27\frac{456}{1,000}$.

It should be pretty clear by now that a fraction having a denominator of 10, or 100, or 1,000 (or 10,000 or 100,000 or whatever) can easily be rewritten as a decimal fraction. Thus, $\frac{7}{10}$ is 0.7, $\frac{13}{100}$ is 0.13, $\frac{5}{1,000}$ is 0.005, and $24\frac{9}{100}$ is 24.09. But what to do about, say, $\frac{5}{8}$? Dead easy! Just *perform the division*.

$$
\begin{array}{r}
0.625 \\
8\overline{)5.000} \\
48 \\
\hline
20 \\
16 \\
\hline
40
\end{array}
$$

To return briefly to the business of ratios, you should now be able to see that by carrying out the division implied by the fraction $\frac{29}{13}$, you wind up with (approximately) 2.23. That is, $29 \div 13 \cong 2.23$, and that's where the 2.23:1 comes from, $\frac{29}{13} \cong \frac{2.23}{1}$ ("$\cong$" means "equals approximately").

Adding and Subtracting Decimal Fractions

Some of the real advantages of working with decimal fractions show up when adding or subtracting. It's absolutely straightforward—just do it exactly the same as whole numbers, but make sure the numbers are arranged so that all the decimal points lie in a single vertical line, as follows:

$$
\begin{array}{r}
210.562 \\
+31.86 \\
+1,752.413 \\
+1.94161 \\
+0.3125 \\
\hline
1,997.08911
\end{array}
$$

The only way you can go wrong is by failing to line up the decimal points correctly.

It's the same deal when subtracting decimals, but when you encounter a situation where you have a string of decimal fractions, some to be added and

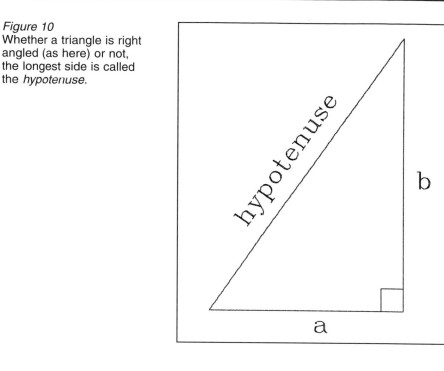

Figure 10
Whether a triangle is right angled (as here) or not, the longest side is called the *hypotenuse*.

others to be subtracted, then a smart way to tackle the situation is to separate out the "pluses" from the "minuses." Add all the pluses together; then, separately, add up all the minuses. Now subtract the total of the minuses from the total of the pluses, like so:

Problem as it exists:

147.21
+8.316
+21.8
-61.78
+473.58
-17.0

Sort pluses and minuses, and add each group separately:

147.21	
+8.316	
+21.8	-61.78
+473.58	-17.0
650.906	-78.78

Then subtract total of minuses from total of pluses:

650.906
-78.78
572.126

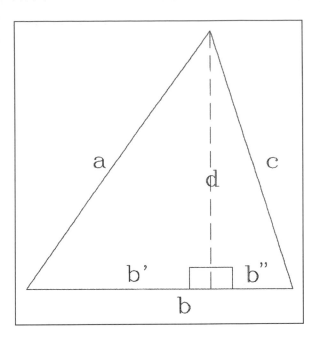

Figure 11
Any triangle can be broken down into two right-angled triangles.

Multiplying and Dividing Decimal Fractions

Multiplying decimal fractions together is also done just exactly as with whole numbers, as follows:

$$
\begin{array}{r}
26.35 \\
\times 7.212 \\
\hline
190.03620
\end{array}
$$

Here, you ignore the position(s) of the decimal point(s) and just line the two numbers up as when multiplying whole numbers, that is, with the last digits of each number directly above and below each other. Carry through the multiplication, completely ignoring the decimal points, as if each was a whole number. After you are done, count the number of digits after the decimal place in *both* numbers (here, there are two in "26.35", and three in "7.212"), and add those together (here, five). Starting at the right-hand end, count left that number of digits and stick the decimal point in place.

If this were a straight *mathematical* exercise, then 190.03620 would be the correct answer. But if the two numbers, 26.35 and 7.212, were measurements, say the length and width of something, in inches, then something weird has happened: we have obtained an answer for the area (length × width = area) that is stated accurate to *five* decimal places, even though we have only recorded the measurements to two and three decimal places. To avoid implying a level of accuracy far beyond our ability to measure (or at least far beyond the accuracy inherent in the numbers given), we have to round the answer down to the number of decimal places in the least accurate measurement. Thus, 190.03620 would be rounded down to 190.04.

The position of the decimal place also proves a mite (just a mite) troublesome when dividing decimal fractions. Here, the trick is to multiply the *divisor* (that's the name for the number doing the dividing) by 10, or 100, or 1,000, or whatever it takes to turn it into a whole number, and multiply the *dividend* (the number being divided) by the same amount. For example, say we want to divide 23.14 into 149.8. First we multiply 23.14 by 100, to turn it into 2,314. Then we do the same with 149.8, giving us 14,980. Then just divide as with whole numbers.

If it turns out that the dividend has more digits after the decimal place than the divisor does, then the answer will have a decimal point in it, too, located the same number of places from the right-hand end as in the dividend. For example:

$$
\begin{array}{r}
0.335 \\
278\overline{)93.210} \\
83\,4 \\
\hline
9\,81 \\
8\,34 \\
\hline
1\,470 \\
1\,390 \\
\hline
80
\end{array}
$$

Percentages

Almost all the trouble people have with the idea of percentages would disappear if they just stopped for a moment and thought about the word *percent*. There are two parts to this: *per* and *cent*. *Per* is a Latin word meaning "for each," as in "Limit One *Per* Customer"; *cent* is also from the Latin word *centum*, meaning "one hundred." (How many cents are there in a dollar, hmm?) Thus, *percent* means "for each one hundred." So, 25 percent is 25 for each 100; 66 percent is 66 for each 100, and so on.

Twenty-five percent (25%) is exactly the same thing as 0.25 or $\frac{25}{100}$ (which you should recognize as being the same thing as $\frac{1}{4}$), and 66% is $\frac{66}{100}$ (which can be simplified to $\frac{33}{50}$, if you like).

To convert a decimal fraction to a percentage, just move the decimal place two spaces to the right, and add the "%" sign. Thus, 0.48 is 48%, 1.602 is 160.2%, and so on.

Powers, Exponents, and Roots

Those funny little numbers above and to the right of other numbers are called *exponents*. The little "3" in 4^3 is an exponent. (The "4," by the way, is called the *base*.) An exponent indicates the number of times the base should be

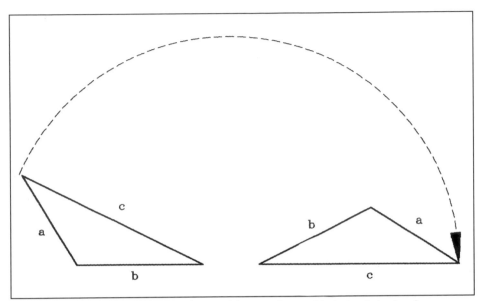

Figure 12: Sometimes much head scratching can be avoided simply by turning things around.

multiplied by itself. Thus, 4^3 means $4 \times 4 \times 4$, so 4^3 is 64. Likewise, 6^2 is 36 (6×6). But why even bother? Why write "6^2" when you could just as easily write "36"? There are at least a couple of situations where exponents are either more convenient than writing out an ordinary number, or else are completely unavoidable.

The first is when the exponent does not apply to a number at all, but rather to a term in an algebraic equation. If that last sentence makes you nervous, relax . . . the jargon is more intimidating than the reality. We will be talking about algebra and equations at greater length below.

The other place where exponents are handy is when you are dealing with a number that has a few digits up front, followed by a long string of zeroes, or a decimal fraction with a long string of zeroes ahead of a short sequence of digits. In each case, as you should now realize, what you are dealing with can be thought of as a whole number either multiplied or divided by some multiple of ten. Thus, 30,000,000 is 3 multiplied by 10,000,000, and 0.000256 is 256 divided by 1,000,000. Now, writing "$3 \times 10,000,000$" makes even less sense (and takes more space and is harder to read) than writing "30,000,000."

As explained above, however, an exponent indicates the number of times the base gets multiplied together, and in this connection ten is a rather special case. 10×10 (10^2) is 100, and $10 \times 10 \times 10$ (10^3) is 1,000, and $10 \times 10 \times 10 \times 10$ (10^4) is 10,000, and so on. But look again—100 (10^2) has *two* zeroes in it, 1,000 (10^3) has three, etc. Moral: *When the base is 10, the exponent automatically indicates the number of zeroes after the 1!* (Yes, 10^1 is simply 10.) So, we can represent the

17

"10,000,000" in "3×10,000,000" as the exponent "7," for the seven zeroes, so 30,000,000 can be written as 3×10^7. This is not only quicker and easier to write and to read, but in many cases we can avoid having to write down rows and rows of zeroes, or punch long strings of them into a calculator, whenever we have to perform a multiplication involving such numbers.

3×10^7, by the way, is pronounced "three times ten to the seventh," which is a slightly shorter form of "three times ten to the seventh power"—an exponent is said to indicate the *power* to which a number is *raised*. In the same way, 10^5 would be "ten to the fifth," 2×10^4 is "two times ten to the fourth," and so on. The exceptions are 10^2 and 10^3, or for that matter *any* number raised to the second or third power. Although "raised to the second power" is not technically incorrect, short expressions have come into being for these two most common powers: Anything raised to the second power is said to be *squared*, thus 3^2 is read as "three squared"; and anything raised to the third power is said to be *cubed*, thus 4^3 is "four cubed."

Exponents do not have to be whole, positive numbers. They can be fractions, or negative numbers, or for that matter, negative fractions. A negative exponent indicates the *reciprocal* of the base raised to the power indicated by the exponent. Reciprocal means 1 divided by (or "one over") the number. Confused? Here are a few examples:

$$7^{-2} = \frac{1}{7^2} = \frac{1}{49}$$

$$4^{-3} = \frac{1}{4^3} = \frac{1}{64}$$

$$2^{-5} = \frac{1}{2^5} = \frac{1}{32}$$

We mentioned that exponents can also be fractions, but before we can explain further, we have to make a little side trip into "roots."

Roots

The easiest example of a *root* is the *square root*. The square root of a number is the number that, when multiplied by itself, gives the original number. The square root of 9 is 3, because $3 \times 3 = 9$. Likewise, the square root of 4 is 2, etc. In the same way, the *cube root* of a number is that number which, when multiplied together *three* times, gives the original number. Thus, the cube root of 27 is 3 ($3 \times 3 \times 3 = 27$), and the cube root of 125 is 5, and so on.

Roots are commonly indicated by the "root sign," which looks like a long division bracket with a little hook on it, like this: $\sqrt{\ }$. If the symbol appears just as shown here, then it indicates a *square* root. Other roots are indicated by a small figure (a bit like an exponent) just above the "hook" on the

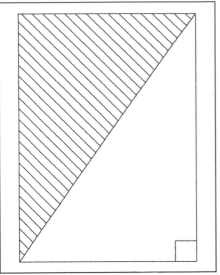

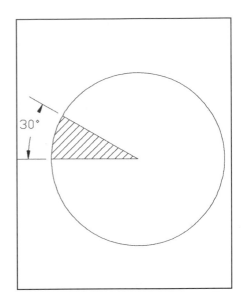

Figure 13: Here's a graphic "explanation" of why the area of a triangle is one-half of the base times the height.

Figure 14: The area of a "pie-shaped" segment of a circle is a fraction of the whole circle's area. The size of the fraction is the length of the arc, in degrees, divided by 360.

root sign, thus: $\sqrt[3]{}$, $\sqrt[4]{}$, $\sqrt[5]{}$, etc. Accordingly, $\sqrt[3]{}$ indicates a cube root, while $\sqrt[4]{}$, $\sqrt[5]{}$, etc., indicate, and are pronounced as, *fourth* root, *fifth* root, etc.

There is a long-hand method for working out square roots, but the procedure is so horribly tedious that only someone whose calculator has died and is truly desperate would bother. And there is an even more tiresome one for working out cube roots, while fourth roots are square roots of square roots (think about it), and so can also be handled long-hand. I have neither worked out a square root long-hand nor seen it done by anyone in at least 20 years. Almost everyone these days has a calculator that can compute square roots, at least. Tables of roots can also be found in some math, science, or engineering handbooks. (And if you want to read about how to calculate roots using logarithms or a slide rule, you can go write your own math book!)

OK, now we can return to fractional exponents, because fractional exponents are roots! $16^{\frac{1}{2}}$ means exactly the same thing as $\sqrt{16}$—the square root of 16. In the same way, $27^{\frac{1}{3}} = \sqrt[3]{27} = 3$, and $64^{\frac{1}{6}} = \sqrt[6]{64} = 2$, and so on.

Before you can add or subtract numbers that have exponents, you have to "expand" the number, to get rid of the exponent. Thus, you can't directly add $4^2 + 3^3$, or subtract $4^2 - 3^3$; you have to first convert the 4^2 into 16 and the 3^3 into 27. The same is generally true when multiplying or dividing numbers that have exponents, with one exception: If the base numbers are the same but the exponents are different, such as $10^4 + 10^3$, then you can

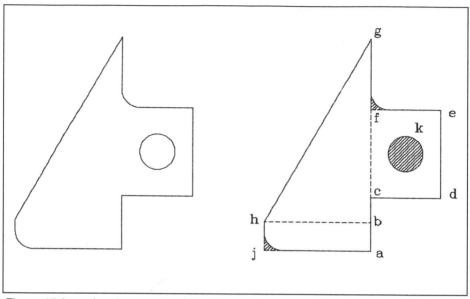

Figure 15: Irregular shapes can often be broken down into multiple simpler shapes, which helps when calculating areas.

perform the multiplication by simply *adding* the exponents. Thus, $10^4 \times 10^3 = 10^7 = 10,000,000$. Similarly, identical bases carrying exponents can be divided by *subtracting* exponents. Thus, $4^5 \div 4^3 = 4^2$.

Algebra

Algebra is simply arithmetic with letters. The letters, called *variables*, are just shorthand symbols that save a lot of writing and make doing the arithmetic easier. For example, in words we might say "the diameter of a circle is twice its radius." In algebraic notation that would be written "$D = 2r$"; the D stands for "diameter," and the r stands for "radius." The letters chosen to "stand for" certain values are often (though definitely not always) the first letter of the word you would use to name that value—such as "diameter"—in common speech. In some cases, too, upper- and lowercase letters (like D and d) are used to represent values that are different but related in some way. Thus, the inside and outside diameters of a piece of tubing might be represented by d and D, respectively. And sometimes small letters or numbers that extend below the line (called *subscripts*) are used for the same purpose, so inside and outside diameters might be represented by D_1 and D_2, or by d_1 and d_2.

Note that it is not customary to use the multiplication sign "$\times$" in algebraic equations, because it might become confused with the letter "x," which is often used as a variable. Whenever a number occurs immediately before a letter variable, it means that variable multiplied by that number. Thus, "2r" means "2 × r". There are a couple of alternative ways that multiplication is indicated, without making use of the multiplication sign. One is simply a dot, located about halfway up the characters (numbers or letters) it refers to, like this: 2 · r. The other is a pair of parentheses: "( )" around each of the things to be multiplied together, like this: (2)(r).

Returning to $D = 2r$, that equation is valid (true) for *any* value of r, so in any specific case, once you know the value of r, you just substitute that value for the letter "r." For example, if the radius of some particular circle you are dealing with (maybe a cylinder bore?) is, say, 2 inches, then you just plug that value into the equation $D = 2r$, so it becomes $D = 2 \times 2$. Do the arithmetic (2 × 2 = 4), and you've got the final answer: $D = 4$.

While there is no risk of confusion with something as simple as "2r," some clarification becomes necessary when things get only slightly more complicated. What do you make of 2 × a + b, for instance? It could mean you are supposed to add b to the result of multiplying 2 × a, or it could mean you are supposed to add a + b, then multiply the result by 2, and *these are not the same thing*. To demonstrate, suppose a = 3 and b = 7, so the expression can be written 2 × 3 + 7. If we do the multiplying first, we wind up with 6 + 7, in which case the answer is 13; if we do the adding first, the result becomes 2 × 10, so the answer would be 20. Using parentheses clarifies the equation: The first meaning, above, would be indicated by (2a) + b, while the second version would be indicated by 2(a + b).

Arithmetic in Algebra

Variables are called variables because they can take on any value. In the examples above, D stood for diameter, but in another situation it might stand for depth, or distance, or displacement. For that matter, we might choose another letter altogether (maybe x?) to stand for diameter. In any case, a "diameter" can be any value—the diameter of a carburetor jet may be just a few thousandths of an inch, whereas the diameter of a large storage tank can be many dozens of feet. But if D stands for some *particular* diameter, and if that diameter crops up more than once in a calculation, then we can add, subtract, multiply, and divide Ds just the same as we might multiply 2s or 3s.

For example, the overall length of a four-cylinder engine block is the total of all the cylinder diameters, plus the space occupied between each cylinder by block material thickness and water jacket space, plus a similar space at each end. Suppose we let D stand for the diameter of each cylinder, let S stand for the space between cylinders, and Z stand for the space at each end of the block. We can then express the overall length of the block as 4D + 3S + 2Z. If, in this case, D is 4, S is 0.5, and Z is 0.3, then 4D + 3S + 2Z becomes 4(4) + 3(0.5) + 2(0.3). That, in turn, is 16 + 1.5 + 0.6, and that equals 18.1.

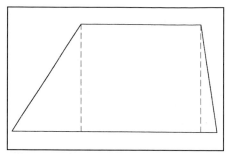

Figure 16: While there is a formula for calculating the area of a trapezoid, it is just as easy to treat it as a rectangle plus two triangles.

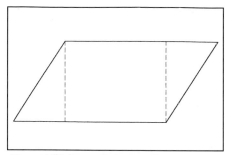

Figure 17: A parallelogram is even easier to deal with—the two triangles are identical.

This brings up an important point: to get from "4(4) + 3(0.5) + 2(0.3)" to "18.1," we carried out the multiplication (to get "16 + 1.5 + 0.6") BEFORE we added 16 + 1.5 + 0.6 to get 18.1. *In algebraic equations, always multiply or divide BEFORE adding or subtracting,* unless the order of operations is modified by grouping symbols (parentheses, brackets, or braces).

Still, the above example is so simple that you hardly need algebra to arrive at the right answer, so let's try one just a little more complex. Although you may not think that you "do algebra," I'd bet you have used the equation (you may call it a "formula") for calculating the area of a circle: "Area equals pi times the radius squared." In algebraic notation, that would be written $A = \pi r^2$.

The first thing to note here is that the symbol " π " is the Greek letter "pi" (pronounced "pie"), and stands for the ratio between the circumference and the diameter of a circle. It has a fixed value of approximately 3.14159, thus π is *not* a variable. The second matter of interest returns us to our point, above, about the usefulness of exponents. In any particular case you would know the radius, as in the example above where we chose 2 inches, and so could write " $A = 4\pi$". But if you are trying to express the equation in general, about the only alternatives to writing " $A = \pi r^2$" are " $A = \pi \times r \times r$", which is a bit awkward and requires us to risk confusion by using multiplication signs, or " $A = \pi(r)(r)$", which avoids the multiplication signs but is no less clunky. And in some other cases, either "long-hand" version would get really clumsy.

Another point about both exponents and the use of parentheses can be illustrated by comparing $c = a^2 + b^2$ with $c = (a + b)^2$. Let's suppose $a = 3$ and $b = 5$. In the first case:

$$c = 3^2 + 5^2$$
$$= 9 + 25$$
$$= 34$$

In the second case:

$$c = (3 + 5)^2$$

$$= (8)^2$$

$$= 64$$

By grouping the "3 + 5" together, the parentheses make clear that the addition is to be done before the result of that addition is squared.

Equations and Transposing

The essential feature of an *equation* is the equal sign, "=". If you want to split hairs, that is the difference between a "formula" and an "equation." For example, we might say: "To find the area of a circle, use πr^2." In this case, πr^2 is a formula. It is a bit like a recipe, or a set of instructions. When we say "$A = \pi r^2$", we are constructing an *equation*. On one side of the equal sign we have "A," which stands for the area of a circle (some circle, any circle); on the other side we have "πr^2". This may seem like needless nitpicking, but the presence of the equals sign allows us to do something called *transposing*, which is a mighty useful thing.

Suppose you are in a situation where you do not know the radius of a circle and are trying to figure out its area. You know the area you want and are trying to calculate what diameter will produce it. You could fiddle about endlessly, trying one value of D after another until you got an answer that yielded the value of A that you want, but that could take all day. Now, here lies the beauty of an equation: The equal sign tells us that the two sides of the equation "balance"—they are both exactly the same; they are (what is the word here?)   . . . *equal!*

Well, if they are both the same, then they will remain the same if, say, we multiply both of them by 17, or add 46.21 to each of them, or divide them both by $2\frac{1}{2}$, or . . . You can do anything you want to one side of an equation, *as*

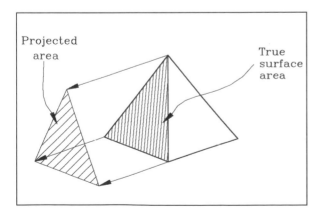

Projected area

True surface area

Figure 18: The apparent or "projected" area of a surface will be less than its true area unless the surface is perpendicular to the line-of-sight.

long as you do exactly the same thing to the other side, and the two sides will remain equal. And that is where transposing comes in.

Let's say you want a cylinder with an area of 10 square inches (sq in), and want to establish (a mathematician would say "solve for") the corresponding diameter. Let's say further that all you have to work with is $A = \pi r^2$. There is no D in that equation, nor any other term that stands for "diameter," but there is an r, and you know (we hope!) that the diameter of a circle is twice the radius. The procedure is as follows:

$$A = \pi r^2$$

$$\pi r^2 = A \text{ (swap sides, to get } r \text{ on the left)}$$

$$r^2 = \frac{A}{\pi} \text{ (divide } both \text{ sides by } \pi \text{)}$$

$$r^2 = \frac{10}{\pi} \text{ (substitute 10 for } A\text{)}$$

$$r^2 = 3.183 \text{ (divide 10 by } \pi \text{)}$$

$$r = \sqrt{3.183} \text{ (take the square root of each side)}$$

$$r = 1.78 \text{ (find the square root of 3.183)}$$

$$\therefore \ D = 2(1.78) = 3.56$$

(The symbol "$\therefore$" means "therefore." Also, in truth $10 \div \pi$ is only *approximately* 3.183, so instead of using an ordinary "=" sign, we really ought to have used the sign meaning "approximately equal"; it looks like this: "$\cong$".)

Geometry

Geometry is the branch of mathematics that deals with the shapes of objects. It is used to calculate perimeters, areas, and volumes, among other things. After counting and the simple arithmetic operations of adding, subtracting, multiplying, and dividing, geometry is probably not only the oldest form of mathematics but also the most widely used. Its origins no doubt lie in land surveying, and it has been employed for that purpose for thousands of years, as well as in carpentry and building construction in general.

Applied to problems of interest to auto enthusiasts, it is used in shop fabrication to figure such things as the shapes and dimensions of parts, bending allowances, laying out patterns of holes, etc. In engineering and design, geometry is applied to determine the volume of parts (and thus their weights), to design suspension, steering, and other linkages, and it is the very basis of "drawing board" work. Indeed, while geometry is almost always applied together with plain arithmetic, and sometimes with algebra, it is to a considerable extent a pictorial kind of mathematics. Arithmetic and algebra can be done using just a scratch pad and a calculator; geometry generally involves drawing lines, even if only in the form of rough sketches.

The world we live in exists in three dimensions, but any drawing we might use to represent part of that world is two dimensional. Whether on a blackboard, a piece of paper, or a computer screen, a drawing is flat. Accordingly, we will start with geometry in two dimensions—what is called *plane* geometry.

Perimeters

The perimeter of a plane figure is the distance around it. Thus, the perimeter of a rectangle is the total length of both sides and both ends.

$$P = 2L + 2W$$

where: P = perimeter of a rectangle
L = length
W = width

Referring to Figure 9 (page 12), the perimeter is:

$$P = 2L + 2W$$
$$= 2(6) + 2(4)$$

$$= 12 + 8$$
$$= 20$$

It should be obvious that a square is just a special case of a rectangle, one where W and L are equal. The perimeter of a square, then, is simply $4L$.

The perimeter of a circle (usually called the *circumference*) is given by:

$$P(\text{or } C) = \pi D$$

or:

$$P = 2\pi r$$

where: P (or C) = perimeter (or circumference) of a circle
D = diameter of the circle
r = radius of the circle

When the lengths of all the sides are known, the perimeter of a triangle is simply the total of those three lengths. When only two sides are known, the solution depends on whether the triangle is right angled, or not. If so, then the perimeter is given by:

$$P = a + b + \sqrt{a^2 + b^2}$$

where: P = perimeter of a right-angled triangle
a = length of one side adjoining the right angle
b = length of the other side adjoining the right angle

If the triangle is *not* right angled, then break it up into two right-angled triangles, as shown in figure 11. And if you are dealing with what is termed an *obtuse-angled* triangle (see figure 12), then all you have to do is re-orient it, and treat it just like any other triangle.

Plane Areas

The area of a plane figure (one that exists only in two dimensions) is the extent of its surface; it is the amount of two-dimensional space enclosed by the continuous line that defines the edges of the figure. The measure of an area is always units of length squared, such as square inches, square feet, etc.

The area of a rectangle is simply the length times the width ($A = LW$). Since a square is just a special case of a rectangle in which the length and width are the same, $A = LW$ becomes $A = L^2$.

The area of a triangle is *one-half* the length of the base multiplied by the height ($A = \frac{1}{2}BH$, or $A = \frac{BH}{2}$) It puzzles many people as to why this is so, but it is easy to convince yourself: If you draw a line diagonally from one corner of a rectangle to the opposite corner, the two triangles thus formed are obviously mirror images of each other, and so must be identical in area. Any triangle thus has exactly half the area of the rectangle that would be formed by "mirroring" the triangle (see figure 13). This should be immediately obvious in the case of a right-angled triangle; others can always be divided to form two right-angled triangles, just as when calculating the perimeter.

Finally, as noted above (we got ahead of ourselves a bit!), the area of a circle is given by $A = \pi r^2$. The areas of "pie-shaped" fractions of a circle (see figure 14) are simply the area of the corresponding full circle multiplied by the fraction of 360 degrees the figure represents. In the example illustrated, the arc *subtends* (a handy word) an angle of 30 degrees, so the area shown is $\frac{30}{360} = \frac{1}{12}$ times the area of the corresponding circle.

As long as all of its edges are defined by straight lines and/or circular arcs (an *arc* is simply a portion of a circle), any irregularly shaped plane figure can be broken down into rectangles and/or triangles and/or circles or portions of them. The areas of "missing bits" can be subtracted. The area of the shape

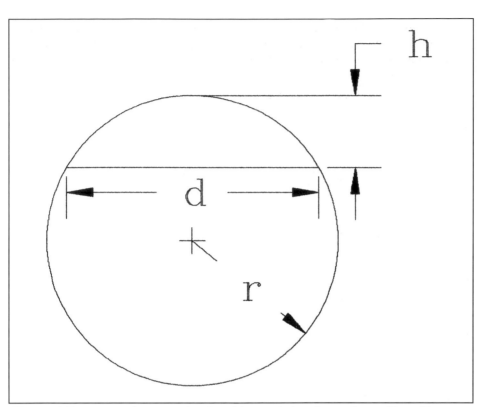

Figure 19: Domes on pistons and tanks with rounded ends require working with areas and volumes of portions of a sphere.

shown in figure 15, for example, is the area of the rectangle *abhj*, plus rectangle *cdef*, plus the triangle *bgh*, minus the hole at *k*, plus the small shaded area at *f*, minus the shaded area at *j*. (As it turns out, these last two cancel each other.)

    There are separate formulas for calculating the areas of trapezoids (see figure 16) and parallelograms (figure 17), but they hardly seem worth the bother as these figures are easily "broken down" into rectangles and triangles, as suggested above.

Surface Areas of Three-Dimensional Objects

    Every real world object exists in three dimensions. The surface area of an object is the total of all its exterior faces—everything in contact with the air. You might be interested in the surface area of an object if, say, you are going to paint it; the amount of paint you need is directly proportional to the object's surface area. Likewise, the quantity of fiberglass cloth you need to construct a part in that material is equal to the surface area of the finished part (obviously not counting whatever you need to allow for trimming the edges). The amount of heat an object radiates or absorbs is also a function of its surface area.

The surface area of a rectangular box shape (somewhat confusingly called a *prism*) is simply the total of the separate areas of each face. As in two dimensions, a cube is just a special case of a prism; because it has six identical square faces, its total surface area is simply six times the area of one face.

The surface area of a pyramid is likewise the total of the separate areas of the triangles that form its faces, plus the area of the base. The sloped sides of a pyramid offer an opportunity to point out the distinction between the *surface area*, as we are discussing here, and the *projected* area of a face of a pyramid. The surface area is reckoned on the basis of the dimensions of its triangular faces *as you would measure them by laying a tape along the physical edges*; the projected area, on the other hand, is the area of the triangle you see when you look horizontally at a sloped face of the pyramid (see figure 18).

The surface area of a solid cylinder is the total of the areas of the two circles that make up its ends, plus the area of the curved outside, which can be visualized as a thin sheet wrapped into a circle. The length of the sheet is clearly the length of the cylinder; its width is the circumference of the cylinder. Thus:

$$A_{cylinder} = 2\pi r^2 + 2\pi rL$$

$$= 2\pi r(r + L)$$

where: $A_{cylinder}$ = surface area of cylinder
r = radius of cylinder
L = length of cylinder

The surface area of a sphere is given by:

$$A_{sphere} = \pi D^2$$

where: A_{sphere} = surface area of sphere
D = diameter of sphere

The surface area of a portion of a sphere, such as a dome on a piston, is:

$$A_{spherseg} = 2\pi rh$$

where: $A_{spherseg}$ = area of curved surface of spherical segment
r = radius of the full sphere
h = height of segment (dome)

or:

$$A_{spherseg} = \pi\left(\frac{d^2}{4} + h^2\right)$$

where: $A_{spherseg}$ = area of curved surface of spherical segment
d = diameter of base of segment
h = height of segment

The surface area of a cone is given by:

$$A_{cone} = \pi r \sqrt{r^2 + h^2}$$

where: A_{cone} = area of conical surface (excludes base)
r = radius of cone at base
h = height of cone

Volume

Real objects, existing in three dimensions, obviously occupy space. The quantity of space occupied is the *volume* of the object. If the object is a solid lump, the mass (weight) of the object is directly proportional to its volume. (In this connection, it is worth mentioning that mathematicians refer to three-dimensional objects with a continuous surface as "solids," even though they might be hollow.) Just as areas are expressed as units of length squared, volumes are expressed as units of length *cubed*, such as cubic inches (ci).

The volume of a prism (a rectangular "box") is simply its length times its width times its height: $V = lwh$. If the prism has an equal height and width, then $V = lwh$ becomes $V = l \cdot w^2$. A "square" cube is the same thing, except that *all* the dimensions are identical, so the volume is just $V = l^3$.

The volume of a pyramid is given by:

$$V_{pyr} = \frac{lwh}{3}$$

where: V_{pyr} = volume of a pyramid
l = length of base
w = width of base
h = (vertical) height of pyramid

If the length and width are equal, then the equation becomes:

$$V_{pyr} = \frac{l^2 h}{3}$$

29

The volume of a cylinder is:

$$V_{cyl} = 0.7854D^2h$$

where: V_{cyl} = volume of a cylinder
D = diameter of cylinder
h = height (length) of cylinder

or:

$$V_{cyl} = \pi r^2h$$

where: V_{cyl} = volume of a cylinder
r = radius of cylinder
h = height (length) of cylinder

The volume of a sphere is given by:

$$V_{sphere} = \frac{4\pi r^2}{3} = \frac{\pi D^3}{6} \cong 0.5236D^3$$

where: V_{sphere} = volume of a sphere
r = radius of sphere
D = diameter of sphere

The volume of a segment of a sphere is:

$$V_{spherseg} = \pi h^2\left(r - \frac{h}{3}\right)$$

where: $V_{spherseg}$ = volume of a segment of a sphere
h = height of segment
r = radius of full sphere

or:

$$V_{spherseg} = \pi h\left(\frac{d^2}{8} + \frac{h^2}{6}\right)$$

where: $V_{spherseg}$ = volume of a segment of a sphere
h = height of segment
d = diameter of base of segment

The volume of a cone is given by:

$$V_{cone} = \frac{\pi r^2 h}{3}$$

where: V_{cone} = volume of a cone
  r = radius of cone base
  h = height of cone

Trigonometry

Trigonometry ("trig," for short) is the branch of mathematics that deals with angles in general, and triangles in particular. While purists may make a firm distinction between geometry and trigonometry, they do fade into each other.

A complete course in trig would occupy a book as large as this one, but the principles of its application are easy to grasp. Essentially, if the length of any two sides and the size of any one angle of a triangle are known, or if any two angles and one side are known, the "missing" angle(s) or side(s) can be filled in. For right-angled triangles, it is even simpler—only one angle and one side, or two sides need to be known to determine the remainder.

The trick to this is a set of mathematical terms called *trigonometric functions*. These refer to the relationships between the sides and angles of a triangle. There are six of them in all, but for most purposes you really only need four. Those four terms are *sine* (abbreviated *sin*, but still pronounced sine, like "sign"), *cosine (cos), tangent (tan)*, and *cotangent (cot)*.

It is not necessary to know what these mean in order to use them; the actual values of these for any angle can be looked up in a set of trig tables found in almost any high-school math text or engineering handbook. Even easier, some calculators have trig functions built in—certainly all "scientific" calculators do. Working backwards, once you have calculated the value of whichever of these relationships applies (see tables, below), then you can look up the corresponding angle. If you are using a calculator that has trig functions, then you will almost certainly find that there is some combination of keys that give the "reciprocal" function. To explain, if you enter "33" on the keypad, then press the "TAN" key, the display will read "0.6494 . . ." (the number of decimal places may vary). This is telling you that the tangent of 33 degrees is 0.6494. If, on the other hand, you enter "0.6494" then there is likely some combination of keystrokes that displays the *arctan* function—that is, the angle whose tangent is 0.6494. In this case, obviously, the display will read "33".

For Oblique-Angled Triangles (Figure 20):

Parts given	Parts to be found	Equation
a, b, c	A	$\cos A = \dfrac{b^2 + c^2 - a^2}{2bc}$
a, b, A	B	$\sin B = \dfrac{b \cdot \sin A}{a}$
a, b, A	C	$C = 180° - (A + B)$
a, A, B	b	$b = \dfrac{a \cdot \sin B}{\sin A}$
a, A, B	c	$c = \dfrac{a \cdot \sin(A + B)}{\sin A}$
a, b, C	B	$B = 180° - (A + C)$

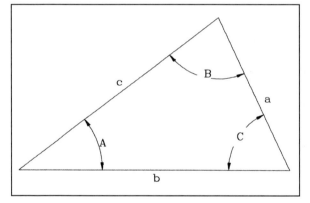
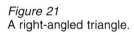

Figure 20
An oblique-angled triangle.

Figure 21
A right-angled triangle.

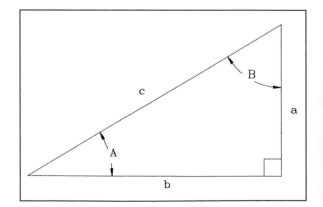

For Right-Angled Triangles (Figure 21):

Parts given	Parts to be found	Equation
a, c	A	$\sin A = \dfrac{a}{c}$
a, c	B	$\cos B = \dfrac{a}{c}$
a, c	b	$b = \sqrt{c^2 - a^2}$
a, b	A	$\tan A = \dfrac{a}{b}$
a, b	B	$\cot B = \dfrac{a}{b}$
a, b	c	$c = \sqrt{a^2 + b^2}$
c, b	A	$\cos A = \dfrac{b}{c}$
c, b	B	$\sin B = \dfrac{b}{c}$
c, b	a	$a = \sqrt{c^2 - b^2}$
A, a	B	$B = 90° - A$
A, a	b	$b = a \cdot \cot A$
A, a	c	$c = \dfrac{a}{\sin A}$
A, b	B	$B = 90° - A$
A, b	a	$a = b \cdot \tan A$
A, b	c	$c = \dfrac{b}{\cos A}$
A, c	B	$B = 90° - A$
A, c	a	$a = c \cdot \sin A$
A, c	b	$b = c \cdot \cos A$

Chapter 2

Engine and Power Math

Volume of a Cylinder

We touched on the subject of calculating the volume of a cylinder in the first chapter, Basics. The equation we provided there was this:

$$V = 0.7854D^2h$$

where: V = cylinder volume, cubic inches
D = diameter of cylinder, inches
h = height (or length) of cylinder, inches

The advantage of this equation is that it uses the diameter of the cylinder, which is how the size of a cylinder is usually expressed. An alternative equation that achieves exactly the same result is:

$$V = \pi r^2h$$

where: V = cylinder volume, cubic inches
r = radius of cylinder, inches
h = height (or length) of cylinder, inches

While this has the drawback that it requires dividing the diameter by two in order to get the radius, r, it has the advantage of working with π, which is built-in to most calculators and so avoids having to enter the value 0.7854. While this doesn't look like much of a big deal, if you have to do it time after time, there is an ever-increasing risk of making an error, just from punching in the wrong value.

Note that the units for length and diameter (or radius) are not specified. The result will always be "cubic versions" of the units used for linear measurement, as long as the use of those units is consistent. In other words, if the dimensions h and D (or r) are in inches, the result will be in cubic inches; if those dimensions are expressed in centimeters, then the result will be in cubic centimeters, etc.

And just to demonstrate that both give the same result, here is a matched pair of examples:

Assume: cylinder diameter, D, equals 4 (so the radius, r, equals 2) and cylinder height (h) equals 3

Using $V = 0.7854D^2h$:

$$V = 4^2 \times 3 \times 0.7854$$

$$= 16 \times 3 \times 0.7854$$

$$\approx 37.7$$

Using $V = \pi r^2h$

$$V = \pi 2^2h$$

$$= \pi \times 4 \times 3$$

$$\approx 37.7$$

To obtain the total volume of all an engine's cylinders (the engine's *displacement*), simply multiply the figure for one cylinder by the number of cylinders.

Compression Ratio

The power and fuel efficiency of an engine are very strongly affected by its compression ratio (CR), which is a measure of how tightly the mixture of air and gasoline vapor inhaled by the engine is squeezed before being ignited by the firing of the spark plug.

Technically, CR is defined as the ratio of the maximum volume enclosed by a cylinder (that is, when the piston is at the bottom of its stroke) to the minimum volume (when the piston is at the top). This can be expressed mathematically as:

$$CR = \frac{V_{cyl} + V_{cc}}{V_{cc}}$$

where: CR = compression ratio
V_{cyl} = volume of cylinder
V_{cc} = volume of combustion chamber

Note that the expression "combustion chamber," above, does not refer just to the volume of the hollow space in the cylinder head, but also to what-

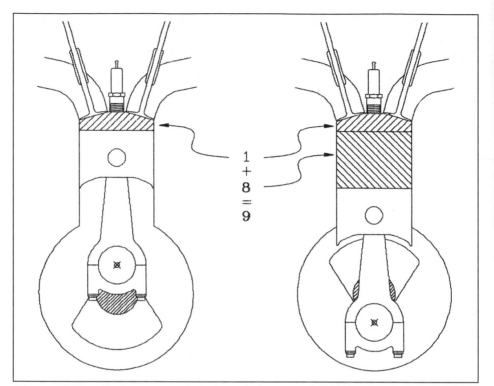

Figure 22: The *displacement* ratio is the ratio between the swept volume (here "8") and the combustion chamber volume (here "1"). The *compression* ratio is the ratio between the total of the swept volume *plus* the combustion chamber volume and the chamber volume, and is thus always one more than the displacement ratio.

ever free space may exist above the piston at TDC, in addition to the combustion chamber proper.

In the above illustration for figuring the volume of a cylinder, we picked an example with a bore of 4 inches and a stroke of 3 inches, which we saw gives a (maximum) cylinder volume of 37.7 ci. Using that same example, let's suppose the combustion chamber has a volume of 5 ci.

$$CR = \frac{37.7 + 5}{5}$$
$$= \frac{42.7}{5}$$

$$= 8.54 \text{ (That is, a CR of 8.54:1)}$$

Note, too, that there is (somewhat confusingly) a related concept, *displacement ratio*, which is the ratio between the volume of the cylinder to the volume of the space remaining above the piston at TDC. At first glance, it might not seem that there is any difference between these two, but in fact there is, a point perhaps best understood by reference to figure 22. If you think about it a bit, you will see that the compression ratio is always the displacement ratio, plus one.

The equation for displacement ratio is:

$$DR = \frac{V_{cyl}}{V_{cc}}$$

where: DR = displacement ratio
V_{cyl} = volume of cylinder
V_{cc} = volume of combustion chamber

We have not raised this subject of displacement ratio as a matter of mere academic interest. While it is dead simple, as we have seen, to work out the compression ratio when the cylinder volume and the combustion chamber volume are known, and while calculating cylinder volume is also a piece of cake, figuring out the combustion chamber volume from the CR and the cylinder volume, using a re-arrangement of the CR equation, can be a bit tricky. If, for instance, you want to raise the compression of an engine to some specific new CR, you need to determine the combustion chamber volume needed to achieve that new CR.

It is easier to figure this out by starting with the displacement ratio, but first you have to rearrange the equation, thus:

$$DR = \frac{V_{cyl}}{V_{cc}}$$

$$DR \cdot V_{cc} = V_{cyl}$$

$$V_{cc} = \frac{V_{cyl}}{DR}$$

Keeping the same value for V_{cyl} as before (that is, 37.7 ci), let us suppose that we want a CR of 10.5:1. Recall that the CR is always one number more than the DR, so the DR in this case would be 9.5:1. So:

$$V_{cc} = \frac{37.7}{9.5}$$

$$\cong 3.97 \text{ cu in}$$

Horsepower

The relationship between power, torque, work, and speed is often a fuzzy area for many nonengineers, so it is worth spending a little time to get all this clarified as we introduce the equations used for working with these ideas.

When James Watt set out to calculate the power of his early steam engines, the basis for comparison he used was the power of a horse, or more likely one of the "pit ponies" then being used to haul coal out of mines. A winch arrangement was used that allowed the pony, pulling horizontally, to drag a coal bucket vertically upward. After taking some measurements, Watt determined that a healthy animal could walk at a steady 2 mph (which works out to 220 feet per minute) while raising 150 pounds.

It is easy to imagine that we might provide the pony with more leverage, so it could haul a much heavier load, but then the load would be raised correspondingly more slowly. Or we might use a winch with a larger diameter reel that would exaggerate the movement of the pony, thus speeding up the bucket's ascent, but the pony (stuck in "overdrive," so to speak) would then be able to pull correspondingly less weight. No matter how you might fiddle with

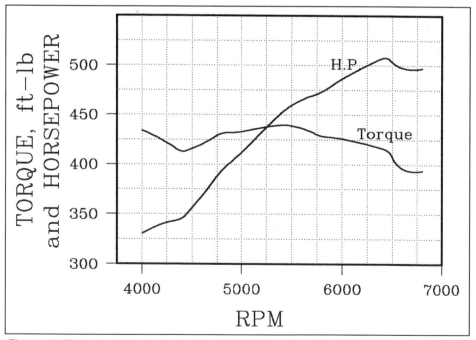

Figure 23: The torque curve peaks when the improvement in cylinder filling due to valve timing effects begins to be offset by the ever-increasing friction losses of the speeding gases. Even though the torque is dropping, the power continues to climb as long as the increase in speed is greater than the "sag" in the torque curve.

the "gearing," all you are doing is trading off load for speed—the *rate* of doing work, the *power*, remains the same. And if what you are concerned about is the number of tons of coal per hour (or per day, or whatever) that one animal can raise from a certain depth to the surface, that is all that matters. It is also the only thing that matters when you are trying to accelerate a car, or attempt a top speed run—in either case what you are trying to do is apply as much force as possible through as large a distance as possible *in the shortest time*.

Watt defined that rate of doing work—150 pounds × 220 feet per minute or 33,000 foot-pounds/minute—as 1 horsepower. The essential idea behind "horsepower" is contained in that last sentence: power is the *rate* at which work is being done. If you apply 1 horsepower for one minute, you will get 33,000 lb-ft of work done. A quantity of work, then, is expressed as so many lb-ft—a force of a certain number of pounds applied over a certain distance, expressed in feet. Mathematically:

$$W = F \cdot L$$

where: W = work, lb-ft
 F = force, lb
 L = length (distance) through which force acts

To return to James Watt and his steam engine, in a typical steam engine the pressure in the working cylinder(s) is more or less constant throughout the stroke. What is more, you can read that pressure on a gauge screwed into the cylinder head, so you can easily figure how much force is being applied to the piston—it is simply that pressure multiplied by the area of the piston. Thus, a piston with a diameter of, say, 6 inches (and so a radius of 3 inches) would have an area of $3^2 \times \pi = 28.27$ square inches (sq in). So, if it were running at a pressure of 100 pounds per square inch, for example, then the total force on the piston would be 2,827 pounds.

At the same time, the stroke is some fixed length, determined by the crankshaft, let's say 9 inches. In one power stroke, then, 2,827 pounds is applied through 9 inches, so the total work done during one power stroke is:

$$W = F \cdot L$$

$$= 2,827\left(\frac{9}{12}\right) \quad (\tfrac{9}{12} \text{ converts inches to feet})$$

$$\cong 2,120 \text{ lb-ft}$$

Many steam engines are "double-acting"—steam pressure is applied to the top of the piston on each downward stroke, and to its underside on each upward stroke. In that case, there will be two power strokes for every revolution of the crankshaft. If we assume that the engine running at 100 rpm, then there will be 200 power strokes per minute. We have already determined that 2,120 lb-ft of work gets done during each power stroke, so in one minute $2,120 \times 200 = 424,000$ lb-ft of work gets done. Since 1 horsepower is defined as 33,000 lb-ft per minute, then our imaginary engine is making:

$$\frac{424,000}{33,000} \cong 12.9 \text{ hp}$$

What we have just spelled out at considerable length above can be summarized very neatly in the equation for horsepower:

$$HP = \frac{P \cdot L \cdot A \cdot N}{33,000}$$

where: HP = horsepower
P = working pressure in cylinder(s), psi
L = length of stroke, feet (note: The measurement is in *feet*)
A = total area of piston(s), sq in
N = number of power strokes per minute

Note particularly that the stroke has to be expressed in feet for this equation to work. If the stroke is expressed in inches, then the equation becomes:

$$HP = \frac{PLAN}{12 \times 33,000}$$

$$= \frac{PLAN}{396,000}$$

When you think about it, $L \times A$, when L is expressed in inches and A in square inches, is just engine displacement, in cubic inches. Also, for four-stroke gasoline engines, N is rpm ÷ 2, so for our purposes the equation can be simplified to:

$$HP = \frac{P \cdot D \cdot rpm}{396,000 \times 2}$$

$$= \frac{P \cdot D \cdot rpm}{792,000}$$

where: D = engine displacement, ci

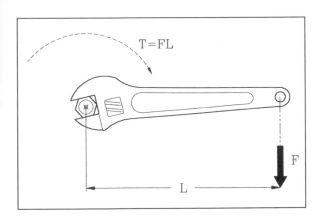

Figure 24
Torque is simply a twisting force. Its magnitude is the size of the applied force multiplied by the length of the lever arm.

Using the example of a 300-ci engine turning 3,000 rpm, and using a figure of 110 psi for *P*:

$$HP = \frac{110 \times 300 \times 3,000}{792,000}$$

$$= 125$$

Where did we get that figure of 110 for *P*? Read on!

Mean Effective Pressure (MEP)

In gasoline engines, unlike steam engines, the pressure in the cylinders is not some fixed, steady amount during the course of the power stroke. Rather, it varies tremendously, rising very rapidly right after the plug fires, then falling irregularly and more slowly over the remainder of the power stroke, finally dropping off to near atmospheric pressure after the exhaust valve cracks open. While there are devices (called *indicators*) that can measure and record the blindingly fast pressure variations in the cylinders of a running gasoline engine, these are found only in large research institutions. So, while $HP = \frac{PLAN}{33,000}$ may have a nice tidy look to it, it seems to be almost useless when it comes to gasoline engines!

But only almost; there is something useful that we can do with this classic equation. If we actually measure an engine's horsepower on a dynamometer (or "dyno"), and if we know the rpm, then we can work backwards to determine the *mean* (average) *effective pressure* (mep) that must have been acting in the cylinders. It turns out that mep is a very valuable measure of the quality of an engine's design, from the point of view of power production.

To understand this a little better, look again at the horsepower equation, $HP = \frac{PLAN}{396,000}$ (when the stroke is expressed in inches). Recall that $L \times A$ is simply the engine's displacement. (And note, too, that in automobile racing of all types there is almost always a displacement limit—the size of $L \times A$ is set by the rules.) That means that, for a given displacement, power is determined just by P and N. But N is the number of power strokes per minute which, on a four-stroke gasoline engine, is simply rpm ÷ 2.

As long as the engine holds together, then, you can always gain more power by running at a higher rpm, provided that P does not get smaller, or at least shrinks more slowly than the proportional increase in rpm. But there *is* a limit to how fast an engine can spin without loud bangs and clouds of shrapnel, and that limit is set by the strength of the most highly stressed mechanical parts, often the connecting rods or their bolts (see "Piston Speed" and "Piston Acceleration," below). And race engines, at least, are already being twisted to as near that limit as the designers dare. So, if you cannot increase N or $A \times L$, then horsepower depends entirely on P, the mean effective pressure.

Just how difficult it is to make serious advances here is suggested by a study of the performance of ten successful, purpose-built race engines, dating from the 1960s through the 1990s. Unsupercharged and running on gasoline, *all* these engines showed mep figures between 163 and 198 psi. Recent passenger car engines likewise show a similar clustering, albeit at lower values, ranging from 103 to 120 psi.

As explained, the actual pressure in the cylinders of a working gasoline engine varies tremendously during a single power stroke; the *mean* effective pressure is a calculated average. The mep—the size of a single "bang," if you like—itself varies with engine speed, depending on how effectively the engine fills its cylinders on each intake stroke. That, in turn, depends on camshaft design and other variables. In general, the mep peaks at a speed well below the speed where maximum power is achieved; from there up to the speed for peak horsepower, N increases faster than P falls off, so $N \times P$ continues to increase for a while. Eventually, however, P starts to drop off faster than N is increasing, and the power starts to sag.

Torque

If, based on the above, you are getting a vague feeling that mep and torque are somehow related, you are right. First, understand that torque is simply a twisting effort—a certain number of pounds applied at some specific distance from a center of rotation—and the result is expressed as so many "pounds × feet" (ft-lb) or "pounds × inches" (in-lb). (It is more than a little confusing that torque is expressed in terms of foot-pounds or inch-pounds, even though we tend to think of it as pounds × feet, rather than feet × pounds. At least this helps distinguish it from work that, we have seen, is expressed as lb-ft.)

$$T = FL$$

where: T = torque, ft-lb
          (*or* in-lb)
         F = force, lb
         L = length
             (distance)
             of lever arm,
             feet (or inches)

When you heave with a force of 50 pounds on a wrench 12 inches long, you are developing a torque of 50 × 12 = 600 in-lb, or 50 ft-lb. Likewise, the push of the piston multiplied by the distance from the crankpin to the center it rotates around (the main bearing center-line) develops a torque around that centerline. And the size of the push is simply the mep multiplied by the piston area. So torque and mep are related for a given engine displace-ment. While they are not really expressing the same thing, the rising and falling values of the two will par-allel each other over the entire engine speed range; without some sort of identifying caption, or a legend that indicates the units involved, it would be impossible to know, for example, whether you were looking at a plot of mep or of torque.

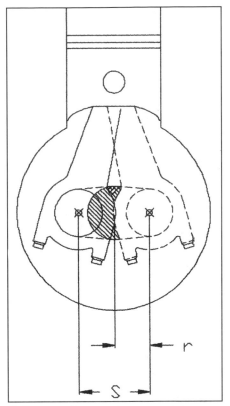

Folks sometimes get answers twice as big (or half as big) as they should from confusing the stroke with the radius of the swing of the crankpin. The stroke is twice the radius.

As we have already noted, $L \times A$ —the total piston area multiplied by the stroke—is simply the displacement of an engine. The following simple equation for torque takes that into account:

$$T = \frac{mep \cdot D}{48\pi}$$

$$\cong \frac{mep \cdot D}{151} \quad (48\pi \text{ is approximately 151})$$

where: T = torque, ft-lb
mep = mean effective pressure, psi
D = total engine displacement (i.e., $A \times L$), ci

Taking the example of a 300-ci engine that develops a peak mep of 110 psi, then:

$$T_{peak} = \frac{110 \times 300}{48\pi}$$

$$\cong 218.8 \text{ ft-lb}$$

If we imagine the engine is turning 3,000 rpm at this point, then we can also work out the horsepower:

$$HP = \frac{PLAN}{396,000}$$

$$= \frac{110 \times 300 \times 1,500}{396,000}$$

$$= 125$$

Recall that torque is a force times a distance. Recall, too, that $P \times A$ (cylinder pressure $\times$ piston area) in the classic horsepower formula gives an answer in pounds, and that L is a length. So, when the three are multiplied together ($P \times A \times L$), we get an answer in feet times pounds, as long as we express L in feet. Taking into account the fact that the length of the lever arm that the force acts around is *half* of the stroke (see figure 25), then with another rearrangement of the classic horsepower equation we can work out the horsepower if the torque and speed are known, as follows:

$$HP = \frac{T \cdot N \cdot 4\pi}{33,000}$$

$$= \frac{T \cdot rpm \cdot 2\pi}{33,000} \quad (N = rpm \div 2 \text{, for four strokes})$$

$$\cong \frac{T \cdot rpm}{5,252} \quad (33,000 \div 2\pi \text{ is approximately 5,252})$$

where: HP = horsepower
T = torque, ft-lb
N = number of power strokes per minute

Let's take for an example an engine known to be producing 200 ft-lb of torque at 4,500 rpm. Its horsepower *at that speed* will be:

$$HP = \frac{200 \times 4{,}500}{5{,}252}$$

$$\cong 171$$

Indicated Versus Brake Ratings

We have explained above that, without rare and expensive lab equipment, mep can only be known by working backwards from dyno horsepower figures. In fact, this explanation is a bit deceptive, because dynos do not directly measure horsepower—what they actually gauge is torque, by measuring the torque reaction of the engine against its mounts. If the rpm is also known (another easy thing to measure), then the horsepower can easily be calculated, as seen above. Likewise, the mep can be figured, as also shown earlier.

But note that these values of horsepower and mep are derived from the torque measured on a dyno, or "brake," so called because the working principle of a dyno is to provide a resistance to the rotation of the engine's crankshaft—to act as a *brake* against it. (The English still use the word "brake" for what North Americans term a "dyno.") Accordingly, such measures of performance are most accurately expressed as *brake* horsepower (bhp) and *brake* mep (bmep). For that matter, the torque observed on the dyno should be termed *brake* torque.

Now, if we did manage to borrow someone's indicator, so as to measure and record the actual pressure in the cylinders while the engine is under load on the "brake," we would find that the average (mean) effective pressure reported by the indicator is distinctly higher than the results we got from a calculation based on the brake torque.

The difference between that value, the *indicated* mean effective pressure (abbreviated *imep*), and the *brake* mean effective pressure (*bmep*) is accounted for by internal engine friction. Although the power is being developed inside the cylinder(s), not all of it reaches the flywheel; some is soaked up in dragging the pistons along the cylinder walls, and in other sources of resistance. As a result, any calculation of power or torque based on imep would also read higher than the brake figures.

Volumetric Efficiency

We have said that the value for the cylinder pressure, P, in all the power, torque, and mep formulas above varies with engine rpm. We also mentioned that the cause of that variation is a matter of differences in how effectively the engine fills its cylinders during the intake stroke at different speeds.

To explain, in a perfect world, an engine would open and close each valve at either TDC or BDC. An engine with valve timing like that would run; indeed, some very large, very low speed engines have valve timing quite close to this "ideal." Once engine speed rises above a few hundred rpm, though, the inertia of the gases entering and leaving the engine makes their movement lag behind the piston. Accordingly, on real world engines the cam timing is arranged to open the valves earlier and close them later, to provide the time necessary to fill and empty the cylinders.

The problem with this approach, of course, is that at low speeds some of the intake air gets blown back out through the not-yet-closed intake valve, and some high pressure gases get wasted because of the early opening of the exhaust valve. Also, there is a point around TDC when both valves are open at the same time, allowing intake and exhaust gases to mix or trade places. The incomplete filling of the cylinder that results from all this will reduce power— that is, reduce mep—and the situation will not sort itself out until engine speed rises to the point where the lag in gas movement grows large enough to match the "exaggerated" valve timing. At that engine speed the mep (and thus the torque) will peak.

At still higher speeds, however, the valve timing will again be mismatched to the lazy movements of the gases, compounded by increasing frictional drag as the gases speed ever faster through the ports. Accordingly, mep will begin to fall again. At first, the fall will be gradual and its effect on power output will be more than offset by the increasing speed (power depends on both pressure, P, and speed, N—see "Horsepower," above) until a maximum value of $P \times N$ is reached. That point is the power peak. After that, though, the restricted breathing will reduce P so much that $P \times N$ will start to decline.

This was referred to above as "incomplete filling" of a cylinder, but in truth, a cylinder cannot be partly full. Except in a perfect vacuum, a cylinder with a volume of, say, 45 cubic inches will always have 45 cubic inches of *some-thing* in it—a gas will always expand so as to completely fill its container, and its pressure will drop proportionally as the individual molecules get spread further apart. What is actually going on is that fewer molecules occupy the same space, so that 45 cubic inches of gas weighs less than the same volume of gas at atmospheric pressure.

This relationship between the mass of air/fuel mixture actually inhaled by a cylinder and the mass of the same volume of gas at atmospheric pressure is called *volumetric efficiency*, or VE. In short, it is a measure of how efficiently the engine fills the volume(s) swept by its cylinder(s).

Now, as explained at some length above, the efficiency of an engine's breathing varies with its rpm, so any measurement of this factor would have to be carried out on a running engine. Obviously, it would be next to impossible to actually weigh the contents of a cylinder in a running engine, and only slightly less difficult to ascertain the mass of the gas in the cylinder by measuring its pressure at the end of the intake stroke. The way VE is actually determined in practice exploits the very fact that the engine is running, and that the air it is inhaling is thus constantly flowing.

The idea is simple: If there were no restrictions to the flow—if the VE were 100 percent—then the engine, assuming it is a four-stroke, would draw in a volume equal to the total swept volume of its cylinders (that is, its displacement) every second revolution of the crankshaft. So, the theoretical air consumption of the engine would be:

$$F_t = \frac{V_{swept} \cdot rpm}{2}$$

where: F_t = theoretical flow rate, cubic feet per minute (cfm)
V_{swept} = swept volume (displacement) of all cylinders (cu ft)

Now, it is simple to measure the airflow entering the engine, using an airflow meter—a housing that is attached to the engine's air inlet and that contains a little propeller that spins around in the passing airflow. The speed of the propeller is a measure of the airflow, in cfm. The VE can then be established by comparing the actual flow as gauged by the airflow meter with the calculated, theoretical value.

$$VE = \frac{F_a}{F_t}$$

where: VE = volumetric efficiency, percent
F_a = actual flow rate, cfm
F_t = theoretical flow rate (for equation, see above)

At peak torque, the VE of street engines is somewhere around 80–85 percent; race engines are likely to show around 90–95 percent. In both cases, the VE will be maybe 5–10 percentage points lower at the rpm for peak horsepower.

Now, the only force available to move air into the engine is the pressure of the atmosphere, and there obviously has to be at least *some* friction losses in the ports, so it would be surprising if a VE of 100 percent could be achieved. Yet there are a couple of ways. Both are arrangements that raise the pressure of the intake fuel/air mixture above that of the atmosphere. One is by use of a supercharger; the other falls under the general heading of "ramming," as discussed below.

Inertial Ramming

Air does not have much mass, but it is not completely weightless; in fact, a cubic foot of air weighs about 0.076 pound. We can take advantage of the

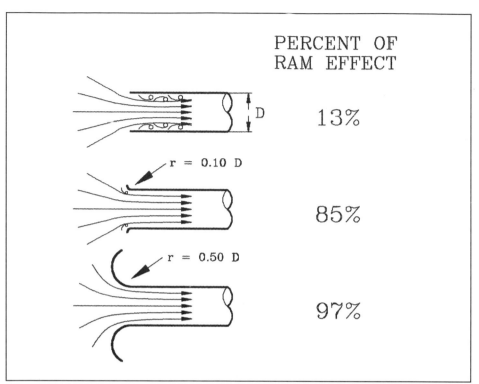

Figure 26: A forward-facing intake converts the kinetic energy in the moving airstream into a pressure rise. The fraction of that energy that can be recovered depends on the shape of the entry.

mass of some of the air "arriving" at the car to increase the pressure—and so the density—of the air supplied to the engine intake. (Even though the car is, in fact, moving and the air is standing still, it is perfectly acceptable to consider the car to be stationary and the air to be moving past it.)

This is the purpose behind the forward facing intake ducts often seen on performance vehicles of all types. In effect, the forward movement of the car "rams" air into the duct, raising its pressure a bit above that of the surrounding atmosphere. The theoretical pressure increase due to this *velocity pressure* (also sometimes called *velocity head*) is:

$$P_{vel} \cong \frac{\rho \cdot V^2}{4{,}311}$$

where: P_{vel} = velocity pressure, psi
ρ = air density, lb/cu ft
V = car velocity, mph

Assuming an air density of 0.076 lb/cu ft, let's look at the effect at, say, 100 mph:

$$P_{vel} \cong \frac{0.076 \times 100^2}{4,311}$$

$$\cong 0.18 \text{ psi}$$

Standard atmospheric pressure is 14.7 psi, so an extra 0.18 psi represents an increase of barely 1 percent, and power output will theoretically be raised by that much. In practice, not even that measly amount is gained. In part this is because an engine's air intake (that is, the entry into the carburetor or fuel injection system) is almost always at right angles to the direction of travel, and a certain amount of energy will be lost in the necessary 90-degree bend in the ducting. There will also be some friction losses in the plumbing.

The shape of the entry to the duct is important too. While the fraction of the theoretical pressure increase actually obtained—what engineers call the *pressure recovery*—can be as high as 97 percent with a smoothly radiused entry, it can be as low as 13 percent if the duct opening is simply a sharp-edged round hole. All told, even with the best design it is unlikely that more than about 90 percent of the theoretical pressure increase will be achieved, so at normal road speeds it seems hardly worth the trouble. Nevertheless, the effect depends on the square of the speed, so at higher speeds the advantage grows. Consider a race car running 180 mph, and assume an overall pressure recovery of 90 percent:

$$P_{vel} \cong \frac{0.076 \times 180^2 \times 0.9}{4,311}$$

$$\cong 0.5 \text{ psi}$$

That represents a power increase of:

$$\frac{14.7 + 0.5}{14.7} = \frac{15.2}{14.7} \cong 1.034 \text{ , i.e., about 3 percent}$$

Piston Speed

Piston speed is simply the speed of a piston as it travels up and down the cylinder. The actual speed at any given point obviously varies. At TDC and BDC the piston is momentarily stationary—its speed is zero. The maximum speed is reached at about the midway point (in fact, at the point when the connecting rod is at a right angle to the crank throw). Ignoring rod angularity, this maximum is simply the speed of the centerline of the crank pin. For example, on an engine with a 4-inch stroke, the center of the crankpin is whizzing around in a circle that is 4 inches in diameter, so it will travel $4 \times \pi$ inches (about 12.6 inches, or 1.05 feet) per revolution. If the engine is turning 7,000 rpm at the time, then the center of the crankpin, and thus the piston (again ignoring rod angularity) will travel about 7,000 × 1.05 = 7,350 feet per minute (fpm). It is worth noting that 7,350 fpm is a bit more than 83 mph.

Usually, though, when people talk or write about piston speed they are actually referring to *mean* piston speed, which is simply the distance traveled by the piston in one minute. How far the piston travels in one full revolution of the crank is simply twice the stroke, and how often it makes that return trip in one minute is just a matter of the engine rpm at the time. Taking into account the fact that strokes are conventionally measured in inches, rather than feet, the equation for mean piston speed is:

$$V_p = \frac{S \cdot rpm}{6}$$

where: V_p = mean piston speed, fpm
S = stroke, inches

Using the same example as above,

$$V_p = \frac{4 \times 7,000}{6}$$

$$= 4,667 \text{ fpm} \quad (\text{or about 53 mph})$$

Many classic textbooks on the subject of engine design—including some that are still in print and that remain highly esteemed—give a great deal of weight to this concept of mean piston speed. Now, it is certainly true that most of the internal friction of an engine is due to the pistons, and that that friction increases with increasing piston speed, but these authorities generally go on to suggest that there is more to it than that. They imply that there is some safe maximum for piston speed (say, 4,000 feet per minute), but that above that limit all sorts of mechanical demons lay lurking.

As in the case of a fall from a tall building, of course, it is not the speed that hurts, it is the sudden stop at the end! The loads on the moving parts do not depend on how fast the pistons travel; what counts is how fast they start and stop. We deal with that in the following section on piston acceleration.

Piston Acceleration

Earlier in this chapter (see "Mean Effective Pressure (MEP)" and "Torque") we saw that, all other things being equal, the power an engine can produce is eventually limited by the maximum rpm it can turn. One limit to maximum revs might be "valve float," which occurs when the valve is moving so fast that the valve springs are unable to force the lifters to follow the contour of the cam.

On modern racing engines and on highly modified stock blocks, however, great pains are taken to reduce the mass of the valves (and lifters, etc.), and brutally stiff springs are used. Here, it turns out that the ultimate limit is set by piston acceleration.

To explain, every time the piston reaches the limit of its travel, at TDC and BDC, the rod has to drag the piston to a standstill and bring it back up to speed the other way—accelerate it, in other words. And we have seen (see

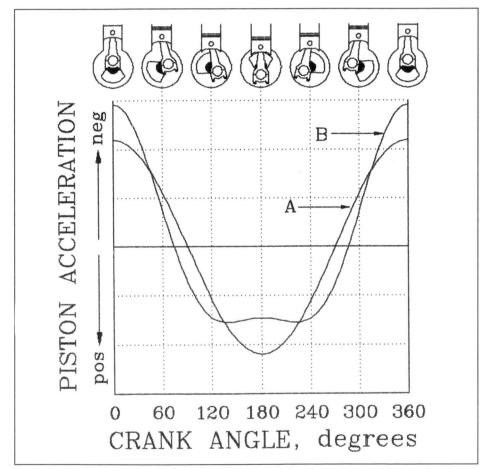

Figure 27: The simplest mathematical analysis of piston acceleration (curve A) only gives an accurate answer if the rod is infinitely long. It isn't, of course, so the "swing" of the rod at BDC reduces the acceleration there, while the same phenomenon increases the acceleration at TDC.

"Piston Speed," above), roughly in the middle of the stroke that speed can amount to 80 mph or more. To accelerate a piston weighing, say, a pound-and-a-half from a dead standstill to that speed in a distance of just a couple of inches demands an enormous force from the connecting rod.

One concern, then, is how much force the rod has to exert—at some point either the rod or the bolts holding its cap on will be torn apart lengthwise by the upward acting force at TDC, or else the rod will buckle from the downward acting force at BDC. Another issue is "ring flutter"—at TDC at the beginning of the power stroke, the inertia of the rings makes them slide upward until they contact the upper land in the piston grooves. The rings, in a sense, try to turn themselves inside out, breaking the seal between the rings and the cylinder wall, whereupon the power goes out the window.

That raises the question: Just how fast can an engine spin without encountering this ring flutter, or worse, blowing itself to bits? In practical terms, the limit is reached at a piston acceleration of somewhere around 100,000–150,000 feet/second². But how do you figure piston acceleration? One slightly approximate but widely accepted formula is as follows:

$$Acc_p = \frac{rpm^2 \cdot S}{2{,}189}\left(\cos\phi + \frac{r}{l}\cos2\phi\right)$$

where: Acc_p = piston acceleration, ft/sec²
S = stroke, inches
r = crank throw radius (i.e., *half* the stroke), inches
l = rod center-to-center length, inches
$\cos\phi$ = cosine of the crank angle
$\cos2\phi$ = cosine of twice the crank angle

The acceleration, in fact, is constantly varying. Odd as it may seem, the acceleration is zero when the piston is traveling at its highest speed—approximately at the midway point in its travel. The most severe accelerations occur at top and bottom dead center, when its direction is reversing.

Note, too, that the crank angle crops up twice in the equation, appearing in both "$\cos\phi$" and "$\frac{r}{l}\cos2\phi$". The first occurrence simply reflects the point we have already made: The acceleration at any given instant depends on the crank angle at that moment. If you were to plot the relationship between crank angle and piston acceleration, ignoring the second term, $\frac{r}{l}\cos2\phi$, you would get something that looks like curve "A" in figure, 27.

That second term, $\frac{r}{l}\cos2\phi$, is important, however. It reflects the sometimes large influence of the rod angularity. In general terms, a short rod exaggerates the movement of the crankpin at the top of the stroke, and tends to minimize it at the bottom of the stroke, as explained by figure 28. If we again

Figure 28
How rod length affects piston
movement, and thus its acceleration.

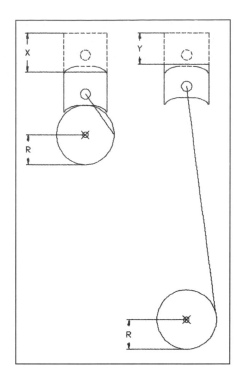

plot the piston acceleration for our
hypothetical engine, this time using
the full equation above, and assuming a rod C-C length of 6 inches, we
get curve "B" in figure 27.

Since the worst accelera-
tions occur at TDC, where the crank
angle is zero, and since the cos of 0 is
1 (and so the cos of 2×0 is also 1), we
can simplify the above equation if all
we are after is the *maximum* acceleration. It becomes:

$$Acc_{p\ max} = \frac{rpm^2 \cdot S}{2,189}\left(1 + \frac{r}{l}\right)$$

For our example:

$$Acc_{p\ max} = \frac{7,000^2 \cdot 4}{2,189}\left(1 + \frac{1}{3}\right)$$

$$\cong 119,385 \text{ ft/sec}^2$$

Brake Specific Fuel Consumption (BSFC)

A small, lightweight car will almost always have better fuel mileage
than a large, heavy one simply because it takes more power to accelerate a big,
heavy car and to push it through the wind. In short, the big one has to spend
more power to get the same job done. That much should be obvious.

But two cars can still have markedly different rates of fuel consumption, even though they are of equal size and weight, and even while both are
doing the same job. That is, even though the power requirement may be exactly the same, one engine may be able to produce that power while burning less
fuel than another. This relationship between the power output of an engine
and its fuel consumption is called *specific fuel consumption* (sfc), and is the truest
measure of an engine's efficiency.

If you have read the section "Indicated Versus Brake Ratings" above,
then you have probably already guessed that "bsfc" stands for *brake* specific

fuel consumption—the fuel consumption as measured with the engine under load on a dyno, or "brake." The units for bsfc are pounds-per-horsepower-hour (lb/hp/hr), that is, the number of pounds of fuel burned per hour per horsepower produced.

$$bsfc = \frac{F_f}{bhp}$$

where: $bsfc$ = brake specific fuel consumption, lb/bhp/hr
F_f = fuel flow, lb/hr
bhp = brake horsepower

For example, an engine showing 280 bhp on the dyno and burning 160 pounds of fuel per hour while doing so will have a bsfc of:

$$\frac{160}{280} \cong 0.57 \text{ lb/bhp/hr}$$

Most engines give best bsfc at full load and a speed roughly corresponding to peak torque (that is, at peak mep). Because the major factors affecting an engine's bsfc are compression ratio and internal friction, engines that produce their maximum mep and torque at low speeds generally show better bsfc figures than high-revving screamers. And high compression engines do better than ones with a lower CR. Considered together, that's a major reason why diesels show better bsfc figures than gasoline engines.

With all that said, it is nevertheless striking that the bsfc of virtually every four-stroke gasoline engine—from lawnmowers, through automobiles, to the huge multi-cylinder aircraft engines of yesteryear—is remarkably constant at about 0.45–0.5 lb/bhp/hr. Diesels, especially big ones, do a little better at about 0.40–0.45. Conventional two-strokes are thirstier (approximately 0.60–0.70).

Chapter 3
Math of Acceleration and Braking

Strictly speaking, acceleration is the *rate of change of velocity* of an object. So, before we talk about acceleration, we have to be sure that we understand what velocity is. Velocity is defined as the rate of change of *position* of an object. If you were here an hour ago, and now are 60 miles away, then your position has changed to the tune of 60 miles in the course of one hour, so your average velocity has been 60 mph.

At this point, you are probably thinking that velocity is the same thing as speed. Not quite, though the two are closely related. The difference is that while speed simply has a number attached to it, velocity includes the ideas of both speed *and* direction. If you drive north at 60 mph, then turn west and continue at 60 mph, your speed has remained constant, but your velocity has changed, because you have changed direction. Confused? Don't worry about it; we will get further into that concept in chapter 5, Cornering Math. In the meantime, think in terms of speed if you like, because in this chapter we are only dealing with things moving in a straight line, and in that restricted case it makes no difference.

Not long after the apple dropped (in a straight line!) onto his head, Isaac Newton (1642–1727) came up with a handful of "laws of motion" which now form the basis for what is termed Newtonian mechanics. Although Newtonian mechanics starts to fall apart when things get very small (as in atomic particles) or very fast (as in approaching the speed of light), these laws remain almost perfectly accurate for describing the motions of objects of any familiar size and speed, from a pebble tossed down a well, to a bowling ball fired from a cannon, to an AA fuel dragster scorching its way to a sub-five second run.

When boiled down from the ornate language of the seventeenth century to the form of an equation, the great-granddaddy of Newton's laws can be expressed as:

$$F = ma$$

where: F = force, lb
m = mass, lb
a = acceleration, "g" (see explanation below)

"g"

If you drop a stone down a well, its velocity increases by 32 feet/second every second. Assuming it begins with zero velocity (you don't *throw* it, you just let it drop), then after one second it is going 32 ft/sec (about 22 mph); at the end of the second second it has gained another 32 ft/sec, so is now going 64 ft/sec, and so on. This steady increase in speed—this *acceleration*—can be expressed as a gain of "32 feet per second, *per second*", or 32 ft/sec², in mathematical terms. Thus, 32 ft/sec² is the rate of acceleration of objects falling freely near the surface of the earth. It is referred to as "the acceleration due to gravity," or "one gravity of acceleration"; common shorthand turns this into "1 g".

So, we return to $F = ma$. The essential point here is perhaps most easily grasped if we transpose this equation to $a = \frac{F}{m}$, which tells us (or should) that acceleration is proportional to the force applied, and inversely proportional to the mass that has to be accelerated. The greater the force for a given mass, the more rapid the acceleration; the greater the mass for a given force, the slower the acceleration.

Let's take the example of a 2,500-pound automobile that is accelerating at 16 ft/sec², or 0.5 g. The force that must be acting to achieve that acceleration is:

$$F = ma$$

$$= 2{,}500 \times 0.5$$

$$= 1{,}250 \text{ lb}$$

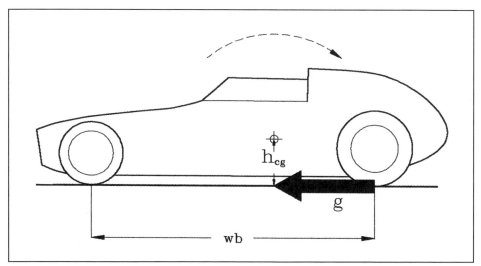

Figure 29: The force that accelerates a car arises at ground level, while the vehicle's mass center is some distance above. The offset between these two creates an overturning moment that increases the load on the rear wheels and reduces it at the front.

We can use the equation in its transposed form to answer a question like "how fast will a 1,700-pound car accelerate if we apply 1,100 pounds of force to it?" as follows:

$$a = \frac{F}{m}$$

$$= \frac{1,100}{1,700}$$

$$\cong 0.65 \text{ g, or about } 20.7 \text{ ft/sec}^2 \ (32 \times 0.65 \cong 20.7)$$

The acceleration due to gravity is a natural phenomenon that results from the size and mass of the earth. An 8-ounce hammer weighs what it does because the earth is attempting to pull that mass—that amount of steel and hickory—downward with a force of 8 ounces. So when you let go of the hammer, there is 8 ounces of force acting on 8 ounces of hammer. On the Moon, the much smaller mass and diameter of that satellite combine to yield an acceleration due to the local (the Moon's) gravity of about one-sixth of that near the surface of the earth, about 5.3 ft/sec². The same hammer would "weigh" just about $1\frac{1}{3}$ ounces, so now there is just $1\frac{1}{3}$ ounces of force accelerating 8 ounces of hammer. And in outer space, well away from the gravitational pull of any planet, there is no gravity at all, so the hammer would "weigh" nothing. Yet $F = \frac{m}{a}$ would still apply—that same hammer would accelerate at 16 ft/sec² if we applied a force of 4 ounces to it, say by stretching a bungee cord a certain distance and using it to catapult the hammer.

The next set of four equations avoid the concept of "g". They express acceleration in terms of feet-per-second-squared (ft/sec²), rather than g. To convert ft/sec² to g, just divide by 32.

These four equations come in very handy when dealing with accelerations of all sorts, including *negative* accelerations (e.g., braking, discussed below) and cornering accelerations (discussed in chapter 5, Cornering Math). The third and fourth equations are two of the few that I carry around in my head. I make frequent use of them. Here's the whole set:

$$v = u + at$$

$$v^2 = u^2 + 2as$$

$$s = ut + \left(\tfrac{1}{2}at^2\right)$$

$$s = \left(\frac{u + v}{2}\right)t$$

where: v = final velocity, ft/sec
u = initial velocity, ft/sec
s = distance, ft
t = time, seconds
a = acceleration, ft/sec²

Equation 3-2 is the one to use when you know the initial velocity, the rate of acceleration, and the time involved, and want to figure out the final speed. An example: if your initial velocity is 30 ft/sec (about 20 mph), and you accelerate at a constant rate of 25 ft/sec² for 5 seconds, then your final velocity will be:

$$v = u + at$$

$$= 30 + 25(5)$$

$$= 30 + 125$$

$$= 155 \text{ ft/sec (about 106 mph)}$$

If, as before, you want to figure out the final velocity, and you know the initial velocity and the rate of acceleration, but this time you know the *distance* the acceleration acts over, rather than the *time*, then equation 3-3 is the one to use. For example, suppose the initial velocity is zero, the average acceleration is 32 ft/sec², and the distance over which the acceleration acts is 1,320 feet ($\frac{1}{4}$ mile), then:

$$v^2 = u^2 + 2as$$

$$v^2 = (0^2) + (2 \times 32 \times 1{,}320)$$

$$v^2 = 84{,}480$$

$$v = \sqrt{84{,}480}$$

$$\cong 291 \text{ ft/sec (about 198 mph)}$$

The above example makes clear that, starting with an initial velocity of zero, an acceleration of 32 ft/sec², 1 g, applied over a distance of 1,320 feet, yields a final velocity of just under 200 mph. Now, acceleration from a standing start over a distance of $\frac{1}{4}$ mile exactly describes what a drag race car does, and while 200 mph is damned fast by everyday standards, that speed is routinely exceeded by dozens—perhaps hundreds—of drag race competitors every weekend across North America. Yet in 1964, when the "200 mph barrier" was first broken (by Don Garlits), figures in white lab coats emerged from the woodwork brandishing slide rules, announcing that this was impossible—nothing propelled by rubber tires could accelerate faster than this "free-fall" rate of 32 ft/sec². They were obviously wrong; we will return to why this mistaken idea was so firmly held under "Friction and Traction," below.

Equation 3-4 is for use when you know the initial velocity, the acceleration, and the time over which the acceleration acts, and want to know the *distance*. For example, if a drag car starting from rest is accelerating at 60 ft/sec², how far has it traveled in 3 seconds?

$$s = ut + \left(\tfrac{1}{2}at^2\right)$$

$$= (0 \cdot 3) + \left(\frac{60(3^2)}{2}\right)$$

$$= 0 + \left(\frac{60(9)}{2}\right)$$

$$= \frac{540}{2}$$

$$= 270 \text{ ft}$$

Equation 3-5 pretty much states the obvious. $\left(\frac{u + v}{2}\right)$ is the initial velocity plus the final velocity, divided by two—in other words, the *average* of the two. That average velocity multiplied by the time, t, gives the distance traveled, s. This is like saying if you average 30 mph for an hour, you go 30 miles. It's true, and it should be obvious.

Friction and Traction

The argument that a car driven by rubber tires could never exceed an acceleration of 1 g proceeded out of many decades of experimentation on the subject of friction, a force that opposes motion. If you drag a wooden block across a wooden tabletop using a piece of string, the pull you feel in the string is the effect of friction. If you double the weight by stacking another identical block on top of the first, the pull in the string will be doubled. Change the block (or the tabletop) from wood to steel, and the pull in the string will be different, but again will be proportional to the weight being dragged. The relationship between the pull in the string and the force (often weight) pressing the surfaces together is termed the *friction coefficient* for each pair of materials. These coefficients are often represented by the Greek character "mu," which looks like this: μ.

Countless experiments of this sort, using almost all imaginable combinations of solid materials, led to a very large number of these friction coefficients being widely published in tables in engineering and physics texts and handbooks. In these tables, "slippery" materials show low numbers; "grippy" ones exhibit high ones. Nylon-on-nylon, for example, has a friction coefficient of about 0.2: to slide a 1-pound block of nylon across a nylon surface will require a pull of about 0.2 pounds. Dry steel-on-dry steel, by contrast, has a value of μ of about 0.8.

These friction experiments also led to a number of further observations. First among these is that, for almost all material combinations, the amount of tug on the string that it takes to begin sliding the block (to "break it loose") is larger than the force required to keep it sliding. The initial "stick" is called the *static* friction; the lesser force needed to keep things sliding is termed the *kinetic* friction.

Now, except under conditions of obvious wheelspin (when accelerating) or skidding (when braking or cornering), the portion of a tire's tread that is in contact with the ground is stationary relative to the road surface. Yes, the tire is rotating, so a fresh piece of rubber gets continuously set down to replace the piece that has just rotated out of contact, but the rubber is not actually sliding along the road surface. So, when it comes to tire traction—the amount of push the tire can develop to accelerate (or brake or steer) the car—it is the value of the static friction coefficient that counts.

The static coefficient of friction of rubber-on-pavement, said the tables, could never exceed 1.0. Well, surprise, surprise, the tables were wrong. Whoever had performed the tests that led to that conclusion had never encountered the ultra-sticky rubber compounds that drag slicks are made from. The tires on current AA fuelers can achieve static coefficients of about 4.5! Admittedly, drag slicks are a very special case, but race tires of many types can attain static friction coefficients of about 1.3–1.5; even high performance street radials are capable of 1.0, plus. Thus, any decent tire is capable of pushing the car forward with a force at least equal to the force pressing the tire onto the ground, and sometimes much more. This force is termed the *normal* force, which has nothing to do with the sense of "ordinary" or "usual," but rather is a term from physics meaning "at right angles to."

Now, as we have already made clear, a pound of push applied to a pound of car will cause that car to accelerate at a rate of 32 ft/sec², or 1 g. Of course, the engine has to be capable of producing enough torque that the corresponding linear force (that is, the torque divided by the radius of the tire) can approach or exceed the normal force; so putting drag slicks on a diesel Chevette will not result in sub-5 second ETs and trap speeds over 300 mph!

But given enough grunt from the engine, the tires on an automobile's driving wheels can potentially shove the car with a force at least equal to the normal force. Note, however, that the total push applied to the car can only match the weight of the car if *all* of the car's weight is on the driving wheels. Only drag cars that can pick their front wheels off the ground—confirming that all the vehicle weight is on the rear driving wheels—and vehicles with four-wheel drive meet that condition.

So, assuming enough grunt from the engine that the tires are the limiting factor, the accelerating force applied to a car is:

$$F_{lin} = \mu\left(\frac{W_{driv}}{W_{tot}}\right)W_{tot}$$

where: F_{lin} = linear force
μ = friction coefficient (for tire/road combination)
W_{driv} = weight on driving wheels
W_{tot} = total vehicle weight

Note that the value of (W_{driv}/W_{tot}) is simply the fraction of the vehicle weight on the drive wheels. As an example, let's imagine a 3,400-pound car with 45 percent of its weight on the drive wheels, and having tires with a static coefficient of friction (μ) of 1.1:

$$F_{lin} = \mu\left(\frac{W_{driv}}{W_{tot}}\right)W_{tot}$$

$$= 1.1(0.45)3,400$$

$$= 1,683 \text{ lb}$$

The corresponding acceleration will be:

$$F = ma$$

$$\therefore a = \frac{F}{m}$$

$$= \frac{1,683}{3,400}$$

$$= 0.495 \text{ g} \cong 15.8 \text{ ft/sec}^2$$

Rotating "Weight"

If you are driving an ordinary passenger car or light truck, odds are good it has five wheels—one at each corner, plus one (the spare) in the trunk. Now, think about what happens when you accelerate the entire car, including these five wheels. The one in the trunk just gets counted as part of the weight of the car and its effect is identical to carrying around a slab of cement of the same weight. For the wheels that are on the road, however, the situation is different. They get accelerated forward through space in exactly the same way as the spare does, but they also experience an increase in their *rotational* speed.

If you were to mount that wheel on a wheel balancing machine and run it up from a standstill to an rpm corresponding to, say, 60 mph, the balancing machine would have to apply a considerable amount of torque to bring the wheel up to 60 as fast as the engine can accelerate the car to that speed, *even though the wheel is not moving through space*. The effect of this *rotating inertia* can be considerable: It has been calculated that in a medium-weight race car in a low gear, its effect can represent the equivalent of something like 30 percent of the apparent weight of the car. (Of course, we are not talking just of the rotating inertia of the wheels and tires, but also of the rotating parts of the engine—the flywheel, clutch, transmission gears, and everything else whose rpm depends on engine speed. And we specified "in a low gear" because the engine and transmission parts, in that case, are accelerating way faster than is the car, overall).

For a body rotating around a fixed axis, the relationship between the applied torque acting to produce rotation and the angular acceleration is given by:

$$T_o = \frac{mk_o^2 \alpha}{g}$$

where: T_o = applied torque, ft-lb
m = mass, lb
k_o = radius of gyration with respect to the axis, ft
α = angular acceleration, rad/ sec²
g = acceleration due to gravity = 32 ft/sec²

The terms *radius of gyration* and *angular acceleration* need a bit of explanation. The radius of gyration of a small mass that can be considered to act at a point, such as a small hex nut on a long string being whirled around over your head, is simply the length of the string. The radius of gyration of a complex shaped component, like a tire and wheel assembly, can only be computed by breaking the object down into separate parts of simpler shapes. The tire, for example, can be treated as two parts, the tread and the sidewalls. The radius of gyration of the tread is just a hair less (because of its thickness) than the radius from the wheel center; each sidewall can be treated as a disc with a smaller disc missing from its center. The radius of gyration, k, of a circle (disc) is $k = 0.5r$, where r = the radius of the disc.

Braking

Recall that acceleration is a rate of change of velocity (or, for our current purposes, rate of change of speed). Since the speed of a car clearly changes when the brakes are applied, braking is an acceleration, too, although it seems odd when expressed that way. This is handled mathematically by designating braking (or deceleration) as a negative acceleration. Thus we might speak of an acceleration of -0.9 g, or of -28.8 ft/sec².

Although there are some significant exceptions (like dragsters, and many highway semitrailer tractors and go-karts), most vehicles have brakes on all wheels. Assuming that the details of the braking system are worked out so that each wheel does a share of the braking in proportion to the weight resting on that wheel, then the maximum available braking force is simply the friction coefficient multiplied by the vehicle weight, $F = \mu W_{tot}$. Thus, a 2,800-pound car with tires capable of $\mu = 0.85$ will develop a maximum braking force of $0.85 \times 2,800 = 2,380$ lb.

Since the rate of deceleration expressed in g's is simply the linear force divided by the mass being decelerated, if that rate is all we are after, the whole issue becomes trivial: $-g_{max} = \mu$ (which is why we can meaningfully refer to a "1.1 g tire," for example).

Weight Transfer from Acceleration/Braking

We have noted above that the acceleration capability of a car driven by just two of its four wheels depends not just on the μ value of the tires on their driving wheels, but also on the proportion of the total vehicle weight resting on those wheels. In the examples, we picked a couple of plausible but arbitrary values for this fraction, but it is important to realize that the fraction of a vehicle's weight supported by its front and rear "axles" varies whenever the car is being accelerated, whether positively or negatively.

This complication arises because the force that is doing the accelerating arises at the contact patches of the tires, which are obviously at ground level, while the lump that has to get accelerated lies entirely above the ground. The offset between the line of action of the push and the mass center (center of gravity) of the vehicle results in a torque that tends to make the vehicle overturn—to do a "wheelie" when accelerating, and to tip over onto its nose during braking.

That torque gets *resolved* (resisted) as an increase in the normal force acting on the tires at one end (the front, during braking) and as a reduction at the other end. It is important to emphasize at this point that the center of gravity of the vehicle hasn't moved, so even though the term *weight transfer* is often used to characterize this phenomenon, *load transfer* is probably a more accurate expression. The size of this load transfer depends simply on the height of the center of gravity, the wheelbase of the vehicle, and the rate of acceleration/deceleration. Expressed mathematically:

$$\Delta_{load} = \frac{H_{cg} \cdot g}{wb}(W_{tot})$$

where: Δ_{load} = load transfer, lb

H_{cg} = height of mass center, inches

g = acceleration, g

wb = wheelbase, inches

W_{tot} = total vehicle weight, lb

(The symbol Δ is the Greek letter "delta." It is commonly used in mathematical expressions to stand for "change in" or "difference.")

Thus, a 2,950-pound car with a center-of-gravity height of 18 inches and a wheelbase of 96 inches that is being negatively accelerated (that is, being braked) at 0.8 g will experience a weight transfer toward its front wheels of:

$$\Delta_{load} = \frac{H_{cg} \cdot g}{wb}(W_{tot})$$

$$= \frac{18 \times 0.8}{96}(2,950)$$

$$= 442.5 \text{ lb}$$

Let's suppose that this car, at rest, has a weight distribution of 55:45 front:rear, that is, the load on the front "axle" is 0.55 × 2,950 = 16,255 lb and on the rear is 0.45 × 2,950 = 1,327.5 lb. Under the conditions assumed in the example, the rear axle load will reduce by 442.5 lb, to a new value of 1,327.5 − 442.5 = 885 lb, while the load on the front will increase by the same 442.5 lb to 1,625.5 + 442.5 = 2,068 lb.

Now, the fact that the load transfer depends on the rate of acceleration/deceleration means that the actual tire loads (which is the same thing as the normal force) will vary according to the degree of acceleration. That is why, in the section above on friction and traction, we included the condition "assuming the details of the braking system are worked out so that each wheel does a share of the braking in proportion to the weight resting on that wheel." Any braking system that distributes the braking effort between the front and rear pairs of tires in some fixed proportion will only be optimum for one specific rate of deceleration. Under all other circumstances, the tires at one end or the other will be required to apply a force that may exceed, or fall far short of, the grip of those tires.

Heat Produced in Braking

Most anyone who has ever had anything to do with automobiles knows that brakes get hot when they are used—sometimes too hot for their own good! But where does that heat come from? A moving object, such as a car, possesses what is called *kinetic energy*. The equation for the kinetic energy "contained" in a moving body is:

$$KE \cong \frac{mv^2}{64.3}$$

where: KE = kinetic energy, ft-lb
  m = mass, lb
  v = velocity, ft/sec

Thus, the kinetic energy of a 2,800-pound car moving at 88 ft/sec (60 mph) is:

$$KE \cong \frac{mv^2}{64.3}$$

$$\cong \frac{2,800(88^2)}{64.3}$$

$$\cong 337,220 \text{ ft-lb}$$

If the car is braked to a halt, that is the quantity of energy that gets converted into heat by the brakes, which is why they get hot. That is what brakes do: they convert kinetic energy into heat energy. There are many forms of energy in addition to kinetic energy, and heat is one of them. And while energy can be neither created nor destroyed (outside of a nuclear reaction), it can be converted from one form to another. An electrical generator, for example, converts mechanical energy into electrical energy; an electric motor does the exact opposite. Because energy cannot be destroyed, the heat that appears at the brakes is also exactly the amount of work done to get the car up to that speed in the first place, ignoring aerodynamic drag and other sources of friction.

Now, gasoline engines are not particularly efficient at converting the chemical energy in gasoline into work (another example of converting energy from one form to another). In fact, about 33 percent is all you get; the other two-thirds gets tossed out in the form of heat, either through the cooling system or down the exhaust pipe. Considering just the approximately one-third that goes into propelling the car (and again ignoring air drag), the heat energy appearing at the brakes is also exactly equal to the heat that would be generated by burning the quantity of gasoline that was actually used to get the car up to that speed.

So, how hot is 337,220 foot-pounds? Trick question! The first problem here is that "ft-lb" is a unit of mechanical (in this case kinetic) energy. But

Table 1
Specific Heat of Some Substances

Cast iron	0.130
Carbon Steel	0.117
Chromium-Copper	0.09
Aluminum	0.214
Magnesium	0.249
Beryllium	0.445
Water	1.0
Carbon-Carbon	0.167

because energy can be converted from one form to another, we can, in fact, convert that number of ft-lbs into a specific quantity of heat energy, as follows: 1 ft-lb $\cong$ 0.0013 British Thermal Unit (BTU). So, 337,220 ft-lb $\cong$ 337,220 $\times$ 0.0013 $\cong$ 433.3 BTU.

OK, so how hot is 433.3 BTU? Another trick question! Here the problem stems from our thinking about "heat" in terms of temperature. It is important to distinguish between these two ideas: *heat* is a form of energy; the *temperature* of something tells us (at least potentially) how much heat energy it contains. Why say "potentially"? Because we need to know a couple of other things in order to figure out how much heat energy something contains, based on its temperature, or to know what its temperature will be if we add to it a certain known quantity of heat.

First, we need to know how much that "something" weighs, for the simple reason that 2 pounds of anything at a certain temperature contains exactly twice as much heat energy as 1 pound of the same stuff at the same temperature. Second, we need to know a property of the "stuff" called *specific heat*. The specific heat of a substance is the quantity of heat, in BTU, that it takes to raise the temperature of that substance by 1 Fahrenheit degree. The value of specific heat varies from one substance to another; water is used as the reference. By definition, the specific heat of water is 1.0; to raise the temperature of 1 pound of water by 1°F requires 1 BTU. Few substances have a higher value of specific heat than that of water; the figure for iron, for example, is approximately 0.12. Values of the specific heat of some other common substances are found in the adjacent table.

So, let's suppose the brake rotors on our hypothetical 2,800-pound car are iron, weigh 10 pounds each, and there are four of them (it doesn't matter whether they are disks or drums). We have, then, 40 pounds of iron into which we pour 433.3 BTU. The temperature rise will be given by:

$$\Delta_t = \frac{Q}{mH_s}$$

where: Δ_t = temperature increase, °F
m = mass, lb
H_s = specific heat (no units)
Q = quantity of heat, BTU

So:

$$\Delta_t = \frac{Q}{mH_s}$$

$$= \frac{433.3}{40 \times 0.12}$$

$$\cong 90°F$$

If the brakes start off at, say, 70°F, then their calculated temperature at the end of the stop is 70 + 90 = 160°F. Even though brakes lose heat more slowly than they can gain it during even a gentle stop, at least some of that 433.3 BTU of heat energy would have been dissipated during the stop, so the final temperature would be somewhat lower than this calculated figure. Because the cooling airflow is more rapid at higher speeds, you might suppose that stopping or slowing from a higher speed would leave the brakes even cooler. Indeed, the amount of heat lost to the air will be larger, but look again at the equation for kinetic energy: The amount of energy to be converted to heat, and so the heat input to the brakes, increases as the *square* of the speed.

Consider the same car decelerating from 100 mph (about 147 ft/sec) to 40 mph (about 59 ft/sec). Note that the speed has been reduced by the same 88 ft/sec as in the first case, but:

$$KE \cong \frac{mv^2}{64.3}$$

$$\cong \frac{2{,}800(147^2 - 59^2)}{64.3} \quad \text{(subtract } V_{final} \text{ from } V_{initial}\text{)}$$

$$\cong 789{,}400 \text{ ft-lb}$$

Converting ft-lb to BTU:

$$789{,}400 \text{ ft-lb} = 789{,}400 \times 0.0013 \cong 1{,}026 \text{ BTU}$$

Calculating the temperature rise:

$$\Delta_t = \frac{Q}{mH_s}$$

$$= \frac{1{,}026}{40 \times 0.12}$$

$$\cong 214°F$$

Assuming again that the brakes started off at 70°F, at the end of the stop they will be (ignoring the small amount of heat lost *during* the braking) at a blistering 284°F.

Chapter 4
Chassis Math

Spring Rate

The *rate* of a spring is a measurement of how stiff that spring is, usually expressed in terms of pounds per inch (lb/in)—in other words, how many pounds of force it takes to compress (or stretch) the spring by 1 inch. A rubber band has a very low rate; the springs used to hold up a railroad car have a very high rate. Changing the rate of the road springs on an automobile affects its ride quality, among other things. Springs with a higher rate (that is, stiffer springs) will yield a harsher ride, but less roll in cornering and less nosedive in braking. Softer springs—ones with a lower rate—will do the opposite.

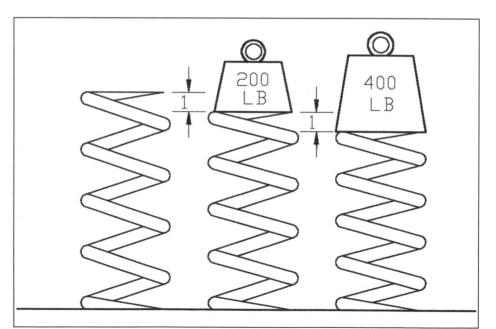

Figure 30: Conventional springs have a linear rate—their change in length is exactly proportional to the change in load.

On most cars, the springs are coils. The rate of a coil spring depends on four factors: the mean coil diameter, the diameter of the wire used to make the coil, the number of active coils, and the inherent stiffness of the material the wire is made from. As it turns out, virtually every automotive coil spring is made from some kind of high-strength steel. Because of some metallurgical differences between the differing spring steels, there is some variation in their stiffness values; while they are similar, they are not identical. For coil springs, the rate is given by:

$$K = \frac{G \cdot d^4}{8n \cdot D^3}$$

where: K = spring rate, lb-per-inch
$G \cong 11,500,000$ (for steel springs)
d = wire diameter, inches
n = number of active coils (no. of free coils ±)
D = mean coil diameter (see illustration)

Consider, for example, a coil spring with an outside diameter (o.d.) of 3 inches, a wire diameter of $\frac{3}{8}$ inch, and having 9 active coils:

$$K = \frac{G \cdot d^4}{8n \cdot D^3}$$

$$= \frac{11,500,000 \times 0.375^4}{8 \times 9.5 \times 2.625^3}$$

$$\cong \frac{11,500,000 \times 0.0198}{8 \times 9.5 \times 18.09}$$

$$\cong 165.6 \text{ lb-per-inch}$$

In learning to apply mathematics to practical problems, it is wise to try to get a "feel" for the elements in an equation, and especially for the size of the effects of changes in those elements. We showed in chapter 1 that increasing the numerical value of a factor in the numerator of a fraction makes the final answer larger, while a larger value in the denominator makes the answer smaller. So, considering the above equation, for instance, we can say (without doing any math at all) that if G or d is increased, the value for the spring rate, K, will increase, while a larger value for n or D will reduce the value of K. Expressed in words, this means that the stiffness of a spring increases with increasing values for the torsional modulus of the steel used, G, and with the wire diameter, d, but decreases if there are more coils, n, or if those coils are larger in diameter, D.

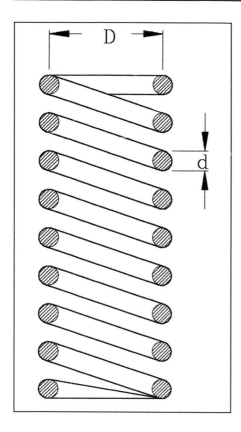

Figure 31
Calculation of a spring's rate involves establishing the *mean* coil diameter, *D*. This is made easier by subtracting the wire diameter, *d*, from the overall outside diameter of the spring.

We can go further, and it is important to do so. Note that the value of *K* will increase *linearly* with increases in *G*. That is, a 10 percent increase in *G* will yield a 10 percent increase in *K*. Likewise, a 10 percent increase in *n* will reduce *K* by 10 percent. But look at *d* and *D*. A 10 percent increase in *d* will increase *K* by 46 percent ($1.1^4 = 1.464$), while a 10 percent increase in *D* will reduce it by 33 percent ($1.1^3 = 1.331$).

Again without doing any math, we can immediately see that while the value of *G* actually varies from about 10.75 million to about 12 million, depending on the particular steel alloy used, the maximum error that can result from using the usual quoted figure of 11.5 million is about 6 percent. At the same time, we are going to have to be very careful indeed when measuring the wire diameter. An error of just 0.010 inch (ten "thou") on a wire 0.25 inch in diameter can skew the value for *K* by 17 percent! 'Nuff said.

Torsion Bars

Except for their use as anti-roll bars (see below), torsion bars are seldom used on passenger cars these days, but they are common in some classes of racing. Thinking about the rate of a torsion bar can cause some head scratching—whereas a coil spring changes length when loaded, a torsion bar, considered by itself, simply twists. (In fact, a coil spring is simply a torsion bar wound into a spiral—when the spring is compressed, the material of the spring wire is actually twisted, like a torsion bar. Accordingly, note that *G* in the above equation for coil springs is the *torsional* modulus.)

The first step, then, is to figure out the rate of the bar itself—how much it twists when one end is wound up relative to the other with a certain amount of torque. Actually, the way this is usually expressed is the number of inch-pounds (in-lb) of torque it takes to wind the bar up by 1 degree. (For an explanation of torque, see "Torque" in chapter 2, Engine and Power Math.)

The rate of a torsion bar is calculated as follows:

$$K_t = \frac{G \cdot D^4}{585L}$$

where: K_t = torsion bar rate, in-lb/degree
  $G \cong 11{,}500{,}000$ (for steel springs)
  D = bar diameter, inches
  L = bar length, inches

For example, a bar with a diameter of 1.2 inches and a working length of 42 inches will have a rate of:

$$K_t = \frac{11{,}500{,}000 \times 1.2^4}{585 \times 42}$$

$$= \frac{23{,}846{,}400}{24{,}570}$$

$$\cong 970.5 \text{ in-lb/deg}$$

Of course, a torsion bar by itself is useless—an operating lever is needed in order to apply the torque to the bar. Or, put another way, the lever is needed to convert the torque the torsion bar is exerting into a straight-line force. Accordingly, to obtain a value for the change in force at the end of the

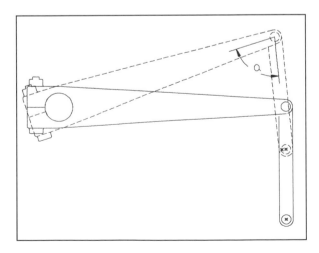

Figure 32
The fraction of the linear force from the link to the lever arm is the sine of the angle formed between the link and the lever.

lever for a given linear movement of that lever, the length of the lever figures into the calculation.

$$K_l = \left(\frac{K_t}{l}\right)\left(\arctan\frac{1}{l}\right)$$

where: K_l = linear rate at lever end, lb/in
K_t = torsional rate of bar, in-lb/degree
l = length of lever, inches

("Arctan" is a trig function that returns the angle for a given tangent, in this case, $\frac{1}{12}$. Most scientific calculators have an arctan function built-in, or you can look up the value in a set of mathematical tables.)

For the sake of an example, let's stick with the same bar we worked with above and assume that the lever length is 12 inches:

$$K_l = \left(\frac{K_t}{l}\right)\left(\arctan\frac{1}{l}\right)$$

$$= \left(\frac{970.5}{12}\right)\left(\arctan\frac{1}{12}\right)$$

$$= (80.9)(\arctan 0.083)$$

$$\cong 80.9 \times 4.76$$

$$\cong 385 \text{ lb/in}$$

Figure 33
Many torsion bar applications use a roller instead of a link. If the roller is fixed in the horizontal direction, any vertical movement will change the effective length of the lever.

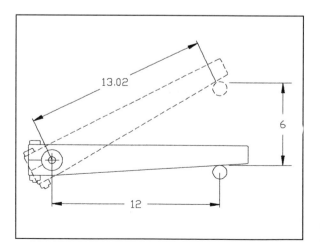

We have spelled this all out as a two-step calculation for three reasons. First, there are situations where we may be interested in the characteristics of a torsion spring that does not have an operating lever on its end. For example, in some transmissions, supercharger drives, etc., there is a demand for a torsionally "springy" shaft, to reduce shock loads. Indeed, every shaft transmitting torque will "wind up"; $K = \frac{G \cdot D^4}{585 \cdot L}$ can be used to calculate just how much it will wind up. Second, some suppliers of torsion springs, having no way to know what length of lever arm their customers might attach to the spring, list their products in terms of torsional rate, expressed in in-lb/degree. Finally, we did it for the sake of completeness—this is supposed to be a book about mathematics, after all!

In many cases, however, it is handier to work with just one equation that includes both the basic torsional rate of the bar and the effects of the lever arm length—something that plugs the two above equations together, in other words. That combined equation is as follows:

$$K_l = \frac{1{,}116{,}000 \cdot D^4}{L \cdot l^2}$$

where: K_l = linear rate at lever end, lb/in
          D = bar diameter, inches
          L = bar length, inches
          l = length of lever, inches

Just to demonstrate that the two approaches give the same result, we'll re-do the calculation for the same bar and lever separately treated above:

$$K_l = \frac{1{,}116{,}000 \cdot D^4}{L \cdot l^2}$$

$$= \frac{1{,}116{,}000 \cdot 1.2^4}{42 \cdot 12^2}$$

$$\cong 382.6 \text{ lb/in}$$

Which is close enough to the answer arrived at the other way. (The slight difference arises because 1,116,000 is "rounded-down" slightly.)

As with coil springs, note the profound effect of D^4. Very small changes in bar diameter have a huge effect on the spring rate. Note, too, that the above procedure only gives a measure of the force acting at right angles to the line of the lever. Because the end of the lever obviously moves in an arc, not a straight line, then assuming that the rest position of the lever is horizontal, any vertical movement of its end will incline the lever. Again as in the case of inclined coil springs, only part of the force at the lever end will act to support the car.

A further complication in many race car applications of torsion bars is that the lever has no swivel or joint at the end, but rather the lever rests on a roller mounted on the vehicle's axle. In this case, not only does the angularity of the lever change with suspension movement, so does the working length as the distance from the contact point on the roller moves relative to the centerline of the bar. Again as with inclined coils, both effects can be dealt with either mathematically or through the use of graphic methods.

Hollow Torsion Bars

To compress a coil or twist a torsion bar takes work, both in its familiar meaning and in the engineering sense (see "Horsepower" in chapter 2, Engine and Power Math). A deflected spring, then, can be thought of as a store of energy, rather like a battery, and the amount of energy that is stored is a matter of how stiff the spring is and how far it has been deflected. (Technically, energy and work are not quite the same thing, but in this case the difference makes no, um, difference.) Now, as explained in chapter 7, Math of Materials and Structures, everything will break if you lean on it hard enough, and it should be pretty obvious that if you twist a torsion bar too far it will snap. (One of the advantages of a correctly designed coil spring is that it will become "bound"—the coils will all close up solid—before the stress in the coil wire becomes dangerously high.)

At the same time, vehicle engineers—especially race car designers—are very much concerned with the weight of everything that goes into a car, including the springs. To minimize the weight of a spring, they try to arrange for the lightest one that will store the amount of energy corresponding to maximum deflection of that spring. They aim, in other words, for the highest possible *energy storage density*, a factor that varies according to whether the material of the spring is stretched, compressed, bent, or twisted.

We have explained that coils are simply torsion bars wound into a spiral, and thus in both cases the material is twisted. It may come as no surprise, then, that the energy storage density of coil springs and torsion bars is essentially identical. At the same time, the maximum stress in either type of spring occurs at the surface; the material toward the middle of the wire/bar is doing next to nothing.

Torsion bars have the advantage that they can be made hollow, thereby eliminating much of the understressed material that is just going along for the ride. Hollow bars thus have a significantly higher value of energy storage density than solid bars or coils. (Theoretically, you could wind coils from hollow wire stock and gain the same effect; I do not know of any automotive application of this.) The bars have to be made just a little larger in diameter, to make up for the small amount of work the "core" was doing before, but overall there is a sizable weight saving.

The rate of a hollow torsion bar can be calculated as follows:

$$K_t = \frac{G(D^4 - d^4)}{585L}$$

where: K_t = torsion bar rate, in-lb/degree
$G \cong 11{,}500{,}000$
D = bar outside diameter, inches
d = bar inside diameter, inches
L = bar length, inches

The linear rate at the end of an operating lever of length l is given by:

$$K_l = \frac{1{,}116{,}000(D^4 - d^4)}{L \cdot l^2}$$

where: K_l = linear rate at lever end, lb/in
D = bar outside diameter, inches
d = bar inside diameter, inches
L = bar length, inches
l = length of lever, inches

These equations differ from the ones for a solid bar only in that D^4 becomes $(D^4 - d^4)$. Thus, for the rates to be equal, $(D^4 - d^4)$ for the hollow bar has to equal D^4 for the solid one. Considering a hollow bar giving the same rate as in the above examples for a solid bar, we first have to decide on a value for d. Let's suppose the inside diameter of the hollow bar is three-quarters of its outside diameter:

$$(D^4 - d^4) = D^4 - \left(\tfrac{3}{4}D\right)^4$$

$$= D^4 - \frac{3^4}{4^4}D^4$$

$$= D^4 - \frac{81}{256}D^4$$

$$= \frac{256D^4 - 81D^4}{256}$$

$$\cong 0.684D^4$$

But $\quad D_{solid}^4 = (D^4 - d^4)_{hollow}$

$\therefore \quad 0.684 D_{hollow}^4 = D_{solid}^4$

$$D_{hollow}^4 = \tfrac{1}{0.684} D_{solid}^4$$

$$= 1.46(1.2)^4$$

$$\cong 3.03$$

$\therefore \quad D_{hollow} \cong \sqrt[4]{3.03}$

$$\cong 1.32 \text{ inch (and thus the inside diameter is 0.99 inch)}$$

The weight of each bar is simply a function of the cross-section area. For the solid bar:
$$\text{area} = 0.7854 \times (1.2)^2 = 1.13 \text{ in}^2$$

For the hollow bar:
$$\text{area} = 0.7854 \times (1.32^2 - 0.99^2) = 0.76 \text{ in}^2$$

The hollow bar thus weighs $\frac{0.76}{1.13} = 0.67$ times as much as the solid one, a saving of a bit better than one-third. Making the wall thickness even slimmer and increasing the outside diameter slightly to compensate would yield even greater weight savings. Eventually, of course, the overall reduction in the amount of material being loaded would overstress the material. (For more detail on this issue, see chapter 7, Math of Materials and Structures.)

Anti-Roll Bar Rate

An anti-roll (a.r.) bar is simply a torsion bar performing a special function. Connected across a pair of wheels—usually the front, but sometimes at the rear, too—the a.r. bar will be twisted whenever one wheel moves up and the other moves down, such as happens when the vehicle rolls. The a.r. bar resists this twisting and so reduces the amount of roll or "lean" of the body. This allows the use of comparatively soft main springs, to provide a comfortable ride, without paying too severe a penalty in terms of body roll when cornering hard.

There is a slight catch, however: Over bumps that affect both wheels together—such as a "speed-bump" across the path of the vehicle—the a.r. bar will simply swivel in its mountings and will have no effect on the spring rate. But if just one wheel strikes a bump, the bar will twist, and in so doing will add its rate to the rate of the spring at the affected wheel.

Although the basic rate of the bar can be figured from the above equations for torsion bars, there is one complication that crops up. While the lever

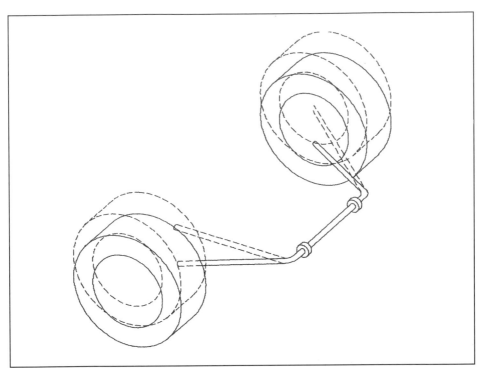

Figure 34: If both wheels pass over a bump at the same time, an anti-roll bar will simply swivel in its mountings. The bar only adds its contribution when one wheel moves relative to the other, as when the car rolls in cornering.

arms that operate torsion bars used as main road springs are invariably very stiff, the operating levers of an a.r bar are usually formed just by bending the ends of the piece of bar stock the bar is made from. These operating levers will bend quite noticeably under load and so will act as springs themselves. (Note that these "extra" springs are in series with the bar. See "Springs in Combination," below.)

The equation for determining the overall rate of this type of a.r. bar is:

$$K = \frac{500{,}000D^4}{(0.4244l^2 \cdot L) + (0.2264A^3)}$$

where: K = linear rate (measured at one end), lb/in
  D = bar diameter, inches
  l = lever arm length (perpendicular to bar), inches
  L = bar length (between bends), inches
  A = lever arm length (along the lever arm), inches

As an example, let's consider a bar with the following dimensions:

$D = 0.75$
$l\ = 9$
$L = 34$
$A = 10$

$$K = \frac{500{,}000D^4}{(0.4244l^2 \cdot L) + (0.2264A^3)}$$

$$= \frac{500{,}000(0.75)^4}{(0.4244 \times 9^2 \times 34) + (0.2264 \times 10^3)}$$

$$= \frac{500{,}000 \times 0.316}{(0.4244 \times 81 \times 34) + (0.2264 \times 1{,}000)}$$

$$= \frac{158{,}000}{1{,}168.8 + 226.4}$$

$$= \frac{158{,}000}{1{,}395.2}$$

$$\cong 113 \text{ lb/in}$$

Springs in Combination

The note, above, about the interaction of the basic rate of an anti-roll bar and the "springiness" of its operating levers is just one particular example of the more general situation of two (or more) springs acting together. Springs can be connected in two different ways: *in parallel* or *in series* (see figure 35). If springs are connected in parallel, they "share" the load, and their rates simply add together. Thus, a spring of 170 lb/in and one of 220 lb/in, connected in parallel, would have a rate of $170 + 220 = 390$ lb/in.

When connected in series, however, each spring deflects as much as it would acting alone under the existing load, so the total deflection is the sum of the separate deflections of all the springs—obviously more than the deflection of either spring alone. The effective rate of multiple springs acting together in series is given by:

$$\frac{1}{K_t} = \frac{1}{K_1} + \frac{1}{K_2} + \frac{1}{K_3} \cdots$$

where: K_t = the total rate
K_1, K_2, K_3, etc. = the individual rate of each spring

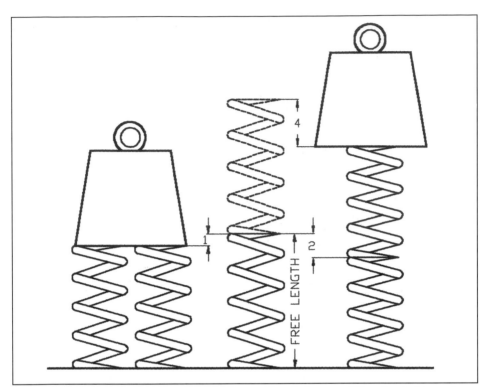

Figure 35: Springs loaded in parallel (left) combine their rates. When loaded in series (right), each spring deflects as much as it would if loaded alone, so the total deflection is greater than for a single spring.

For example, consider the total affective rate of three springs in series, having individual rates of 150 lb/in, 250 lb/in, and 350 lb/in:

$$\frac{1}{K_t} = \frac{1}{150} + \frac{1}{250} + \frac{1}{350}$$

$$= \frac{875}{131{,}250} + \frac{525}{131{,}250} + \frac{375}{131{,}250}$$

$$= \frac{1{,}775}{131{,}250}$$

$$\cong 0.0135$$
$$\therefore \ K_t \cong 73.9 \ \text{lb/in}$$

Where there are just two springs, the above can be simplified to:

$$K_t = \frac{K_1 \cdot K_2}{K_1 + K_2}$$

As an example, consider again two springs with rates of 170 lb/in and 220 lb/in, only this time acting in series:

$$K_t = \frac{170 \times 220}{170 + 220}$$

$$= \frac{37,400}{390}$$

$$\cong 96 \text{ lb/in}$$

Note that this is far less than the rate of either of the two springs considered separately. This reduction in rate from springs in series can be a factor that confuses the issue when changing spring rates. It is quite common for coil springs, for example, to rest on a thick rubber isolator pad, usually to reduce noise transmission into the vehicle body shell. The rubber pad is obviously flexible and so will act as a spring in series with the coil. Even though it may be much stiffer than the coil, it will nevertheless drop the rate of the two acting together. Similarly, some "coil-over" damper/spring units have one or both end fittings in the form of an "eye" surrounded by a rubber bushing. Again, the rubber will act as a stiff secondary spring in series with the coil and so will again drop the rate.

Leaf Springs

Many trucks, trailers, and older cars use leaf springs. Compared to coils or torsion bars, leaf springs have a number of drawbacks. First, they are much less efficient, in terms of energy storage density. As a result, they will necessarily weigh more than a coil or torsion bar in the same installation, if designed to work the spring material equally close to the breaking point. To be fair, some of the extra weight of a leaf spring can be written off against the weight of the separate linkage that is needed to guide the path of the wheel (or axle) when coils or torsion bars are used. Leaf springs provide this locating function by themselves. Finally, some people choose to use leaf springs because it is relatively inexpensive to do so.

Second, in the familiar multi-leaf spring, the individual leaves have to slide over one another as the spring flexes, but because the leaves are clamped

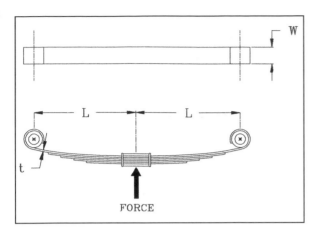

Figure 36
Key dimensions for calculating the rate of a leaf spring (see text).

tightly together, there is considerable friction resisting this sliding motion. In fact, it takes a substantial amount of force to initially "break loose" this *inter-leaf friction*, so over small bumps the suspension will be effectively locked solid, and all the springing will have to come from the tires and from the rubber bushings usually included at the spring ends. Tapered mono-leaf (single-leaf) springs avoid this drawback.

Finally, the calculation of the rate of a multi-leaf spring is an "iffy" business (and a positive nightmare for mono-leaf springs). Any equation for rate calculation is at best an approximation, and should be checked by physically loading the spring and measuring the deflection. Nevertheless, if all the leaves are of the same thickness, the spring is symmetrical end-to-end, and the load is applied right at the middle, then the following is a starting place:

$$K \cong \frac{(2 + \frac{1}{n})nwEt^3}{6L^3}$$

where: K = spring rate, lb/in
n = number of leaves
w = width of each leaf, inches
t = thickness of each leaf, inches
L = *half* of spring eye-to-eye length, inches
E = 30,000,000 (for steel springs)

(E represents the tensile modulus of a material, here steel. Unlike G—the torsional modulus—used in the torsion bar equations, the value of E is pretty nearly identical for all steels.)

As an example, let's consider a leaf spring having the following dimensions:

$$n = 5$$
$$w = 3.0$$
$$t = 0.25$$
$$L = 30$$

$$K \cong \frac{(2 + \frac{1}{n})nwEt^3}{6L^3}$$

$$\cong \frac{(2 + \frac{1}{5}) \cdot 5 \cdot 3 \cdot 30{,}000{,}000 \cdot (0.25)^3}{6(30)^3}$$

$$\cong \frac{2.2 \cdot 5 \cdot 3 \cdot 30{,}000{,}000 \cdot 0.0156}{6 \cdot 27{,}000}$$

$$\cong 95.3 \ \mathrm{lb/in}$$

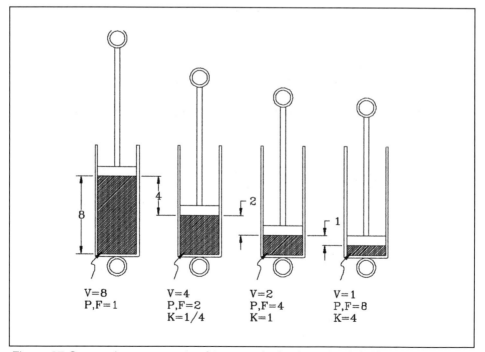

Figure 37: Successive movements of a gas spring's piston, each half the size of the previous one, yield a halving of the volume of the trapped gas, and so a doubling of its pressure. The force on the piston thus rises as the *square* of the travel, so a gas spring exhibits a rising rate.

It is also worth noting that the above only works if each leaf in the stack is shorter than the one above, and by the same amount, as is usually (but not always) the case.

Air Springs

The energy storage density of a spring is simply a matter of the amount of energy it can store per unit of spring weight. An "ideal" spring material would be one that is very light, yet can store a large amount of energy without breaking. In this regard, air seems nearly perfect. It weighs next to nothing, yet can be compressed to eye-watering pressures, in which case it "fights back" with potentially huge forces. And you can't "break" air (though you *can* break wi—, oh, never mind).

Air springs have some other characteristics that are arguable advantages. Very often, what is wanted is a spring that is "soft" when coping with small disturbances, to provide a comfortable ride, but which stiffens up with large deflections, so as to prevent "bottoming."

Torsion bars and conventional coil springs have a "linear" rate—that is, whatever force they resist with when deflected one unit (a degree, an inch), they will develop twice that force when deflected two units, and so on. Now, a coil spring that is wound so that the spacing between coils varies along the length of the spring (or, much more rarely, with coils wound from tapered wire) will grow stiffer with increasing deflections. But this "rising rate" characteristic is achieved inherently by springs that use air, or any other gas. Here's why:

While the details of their internal construction vary, all gas springs can be thought of as a piston in a closed-ended cylinder filled with gas. A trapped volume of gas such as this observes Boyle's law: If the temperature is kept constant, the pressure of a fixed quantity of gas varies directly according to the size (volume) of its container—the pressure times the volume is always some constant number.

Expressed mathematically:

$$P \cdot V = k$$

where: P = the pressure (any units)
V = the volume (any units)
k = a constant number (varies with the units)

Now, imagine a cylinder with a bore of 4 inches and a length of 8 inches (so it has a volume of just a hair more than 100 cubic inches) that is filled with a gas at, say, 40 psi, and with its open end closed off by a piston. If the piston is now forced into the cylinder a distance of 4 inches, the new volume will obviously be half of the original 100 cubic inches. According to Boyle's law:

$$P_2 \cdot V_2 = P_1 \cdot V_1 = k$$

$$\therefore \; P_2 = \left(\frac{V_1}{V_2}\right)P_1$$

where: P_1 = the original pressure
P_2 = the new pressure
V_1 = the original volume
V_2 = the new volume

But the new volume is only half the original volume. That is:

$$V_1 = 2V_2$$

$$\therefore \; P_2 = \left(\frac{2V_2}{V_2}\right)P_1$$

$$P_2 = 2P_1$$

This tells us, if we hadn't already guessed, that the halving of the size of the enclosure has doubled the pressure of the gas, to 80 psi. Initially, the 40 psi acting on the piston area of $4^2 \times 0.7854 \cong 12.6$ sq in produced a force of $40 \times 12.6 = 504$ pounds. Now, the doubled pressure produces a force exactly twice that, 1,008 pounds. The average rate over the first 4 inches of movement, then, has been:

$$\frac{1,008 - 504}{4} = 126 \text{ lb/in}$$

Ah, but look what happens if we force the piston in another 2 (not 4) inches—the volume is again cut in half, so the pressure will again be doubled, to 160 psi. The force on the piston will thus be $160 \times 12.6 = 2,016$ pounds. The average rate over that most recent 2 inches of travel is therefore:

$$\frac{2,016 - 1,008}{2} = 504 \text{ lb/in}$$

And if we shove in just one further inch, the same logic reveals a rate of:

$$\frac{(320 \times 12.6) - 2,016}{1} = 2,016 \text{ lb/in}$$

After a brief flurry of interest in air springs for passenger cars in the mid-1950s, the scheme virtually disappeared, only to be revived on some luxury models within the past five years or so. Though still rare as a *principal* road spring, air springs are rather more common than you might think. Apart from

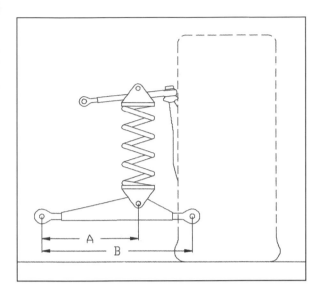

Figure 38
Any "leverage" between a wheel and the spring supporting it affects *both* the force experienced by the spring *and* its travel. Thus the spring rate at the wheel is not the rate multiplied by *A/B* but rather *A/B squared.*

their use as auxiliary "load levelers," every "gas-filled" damper (shock absorber) acts as a sort of auxiliary air spring, and both will have essentially the characteristics described above. In a handful of applications, such as a few motorcycles and top-priced "mountain" bicycles, the gas pressure section of a gas-filled damper is used as the primary spring.

Wheel Rate

For calculations involving a car's suspension, we are more likely to be interested in the spring rate experienced by the wheel, rather than the raw value for the spring itself. Now, if the spring for a particular wheel acts directly at the wheel and is aligned straight up and down, then the two will be exactly the same. But this almost never happens, so the wheel rate will generally be different from the spring rate. Here's why.

Usually, the lower end of the spring is mounted on one of the suspension links some distance inboard of the wheel, as in figure 4-9. It should be fairly obvious that the wheel accordingly has some degree of "leverage" against the spring, so the rate measured at the wheel will be lower than that of the spring.

What is not so obvious is that there are *two* effects of this leverage. First, a 1-inch movement of the wheel will produce less movement at the spring, say three-fourths of an inch. So if the spring has a rate of 240 lb/in, then 1 inch of upward movement at the wheel will only produce $\frac{3}{4} \times 240 = 180$ lb of additional force from the spring. However, the wheel does not experience the full 180 pounds of extra force but rather some lesser amount, again because of the "leverage." The "leverage," in other words, affects *both* the force *and* the travel, so whatever the ratio of *A* to *B* in figure 38 happens to be, the wheel rate will not simply be $\frac{A}{B}$ multiplied by the spring rate but rather $(\frac{A}{B})^2$ multiplied by the spring rate.

For example, if dimension A in the illustration is, say, 12 inches, and dimension B is 16 inches, then if we continue to suppose that the rate of the spring itself is 240 lb/in, the rate at the wheel will be:

$$K_{wheel} = K_{spring} \left(\frac{A}{B} \right)^2$$

$$= 240 \left(\frac{12}{16} \right)^2$$

$$= 240 \times (0.75)^2$$

$$= 240 \times 0.5625$$

$$= 135 \text{ lb/in}$$

With more complicated systems, such as inboard springs operated either by a rocker arm or by a push- or pull-rod and bell-crank arrangement, the principle remains the same: You have to figure out (or, simpler and potentially more accurate, actually measure) the ratio of the movements of the wheel and the spring. This is called the *installation ratio*. The rate experienced by the wheel will always be the basic spring rate multiplied by the installation ratio *squared*. But there is a bit more to it.

In figure 39, and in most real world systems, the spring is not oriented vertically, but rather at some angle. If we imagine the thing laid over even further, so it is perfectly parallel to the lower suspension arm (in this case, completely horizontal), then the spring will be unable to hold the car up at all. All of its force is trying to stretch the link; none of it acts downward against the wheel (and thus upward against the chassis, to fight gravity).

With lesser, more realistic angles, *part* of the spring force will be pushing the wheel down and *part* of it will be trying to stretch the link. There are two ways to reckon the size of the portion acting downward. The first is to look up the value of the cosine of the angle, α, in a set of trigonometry tables, and to then multiply the raw value of the spring rate by that number before going on to deal with the issue of the installation ratio. (All scientific calculators, and many others, have these tables built-in. Look for a function called "cos"; usually, you just enter the value for the angle, in degrees, and push "cos." The display will show the value of the cosine for that angle.)

In figure 39, the angle, α, just happens to be 45 degrees. The cosine of 45 degrees is 0.707, so the force acting vertically downward at the spring mounting on the lower arm will be 0.707 times the force actually exerted by

Back to the Drawing Board

A few people, academics mostly, study mathematics for its own sake. The rest of us regard it as a tool; we use math as a way of solving practical problems. But there are some alternative tools involving no real "mathematics" at all that enable us to obtain a numerical answer to certain physical problems. One good example of this is the use of *graphical* methods—drawing board work—to determine what fraction of a force aimed in a certain direction will act in some other direction. In the section on wheel rates, for example, we explained that the vertical force acting at the mountings of an inclined spring is some fraction of the force acting along the line of the spring, and that the effective spring rate at the mountings is reduced in exactly the same pro-

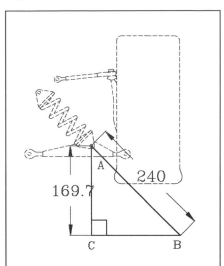

Calculations involving trigonometry may be avoided by drawing board work, such as when figuring the components of a force.

portion. We can calculate this, as described in that section, or we can solve the problem with a scale drawing.

In the adjacent drawing we have represented the spring rate of 240 lb/in with the line A-B. Note that the line is drawn in the same direction as the spring force—that is, along a line joining the spring mountings. You can use any scale you want to establish the length of this line. If the drawing is small, we might make the scale 1 = 100. That is, a line 1 inch long would represent a rate of 100 lb/in. In this case, the line would be 2.4 inches long. We next draw a line horizontally from B toward the left and another line vertically downward from A, so that the two intersect at C.

Now here's the magic part: the length of A-C now represents the component of the spring force acting along A-C (vertically downward, in other words) in the same scale as we chose for line A-B. If we carefully measure the length of A-C we discover its length to be 1.697 inches, which represents 169.7 lb/in. Now, in truth, you cannot measure the length of a pencil line with that level of precision. If you need three-digit accuracy in your answer, you could choose a much finer scale, say 10 = 1 (although that would require a much larger piece of paper!). In reality, we would probably measure A-C to be 1.7 inches, representing 170 lb/in, which is plenty close enough for practical purposes.

Figure 39
The *vertical* force experienced by the lower spring mount equals the force measured *along* the spring, multiplied by the cosine of the installation angle.

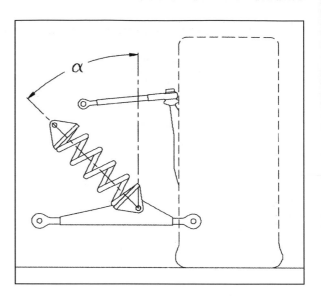

the spring. Assuming the same 240 lb/in rate in the previous example for the spring itself (and ignoring the slight change in the angle of the spring that occurs when the suspension deflects), a 1-inch upward movement of the lower spring mounting point will increase the force at that point by $24 \times 0.707 = 169.7$ lb.

The second way to evaluate the effect of the installed angle of the spring is to do it graphically, as described in the adjacent sidebar.

Ride Frequency

Spring rates, even rates measured at the wheel, do not by themselves tell anything about whether the springing is "soft" or "hard." Sure, soft springs bounce more slowly than stiff ones, but a heavily loaded spring also bounces more slowly than a lightly loaded one. The springs from a billowy riding, full-size sedan of the 1960s would make for a bone-crushing ride when installed on a lightweight car.

One common measure for the "softness" or "hardness" of an automobile's ride is the *ride frequency*, usually expressed separately for the front and rear suspension. This is the rate of bounce, in cycles per minute (cpm), that you experience when you jump up and down on a bumper to judge the condition of the dampers (shock absorbers). Properly working dampers snub this bouncing action, and thus affect the ride quality for better or worse, but this effect is overlaid on top of the basic ride quality that depends on the ride frequency. Stiffer springs will raise the ride frequency, softer ones will lower it.

The ride frequency can be calculated as follows:

$$F_{nat} = \frac{187.8}{\sqrt{s}}$$

where: F_{nat} = natural bounce frequency, cpm
          s = static spring displacement, inches

Note that the effect of both the spring rate and the weight resting on the spring are accounted for in this formula by the value s, the static displacement of the spring—how much it is compressed from its free length because of the weight it supports. A spring with a rate of 250 lb/in supporting a weight of 750 pounds, for example, would have a static compression of 3 inches. In this case:

$$F_{nat} = \frac{187.8}{\sqrt{3}}$$

$$\cong \frac{187.8}{1.73}$$

$$\cong 108.4 \text{ cpm}$$

Typical street vehicles have a ride frequency at the front of somewhere around 70 cpm; the rear suspension is usually a bit stiffer, say 80–90. A ride frequency of 108 cpm, then, would correspond to a pretty hard ride for a street vehicle—say, the rear suspension of a Corvette. Race cars are usually sprung much harder.

Weight Distribution/Center of Gravity

An automobile is obviously made up of thousands of separate objects. Some, like the cylinder block, are heavy; others, like a single sheet-metal screw, are light. Gravity acts separately on each of these objects, but there is some point where all of the separate weights of these different objects "balance out." If supported at its center of gravity (c.g., or sometimes C-of-G), an object will balance. The c.g., in other words, is the point at which the gravitational pull of the earth can be considered to act on the object as a whole. In the case of an automobile, the c.g. invariably lies somewhere within the overall space occupied by the vehicle, but note that in other cases, the c.g. can lie outside the object itself. The c.g. of a donut, for example, lies right in the middle of the hole, where there isn't any donut at all! (For that matter, the c.g. of a typical production car is a point somewhere in the air within the passenger compartment.)

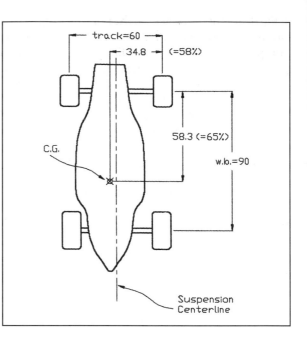

Figure 40
Determining the location of a car's center of gravity in a "plan" (bird's-eye) view is just a matter of measuring wheel "weights," wheelbase and track width, and applying a little arithmetic.

It is not only the force of gravity that acts, overall, at the c.g. When an automobile accelerates, for example, all the separate masses of all its different parts "balance out" at the c.g. (thus, c.g. is also sometimes termed "mass center"), so the *inertia* of the car acts at the c.g. Because the separate parts that make up the car are all above ground level, the c.g. has to be above ground level too. But the force producing the acceleration arises at ground level, where the driving wheels contact.

The result of this offset between the source of the push and the location of the thing being pushed is similar to what happens if you have a broomstick balanced on your fingertip, then suddenly thrust your finger forward—the inertia of the broomstick acts at its c.g. (right in the geometric center of the stick), which lies above the point where the force is applied (your fingertip), so the broomstick falls backward. In the same way, the accelerating car will "fall backwards," which is why cars squat their tail ends when they accelerate. And why they drop their noses when they are braked. And why they lean to the side in turns.

Now, unlike a broomstick on a finger, an automobile is not supported just at a single point, but rather at four points—the tire contact patches. Because a tire's ability to push forward (or backward, or sideways) depends on how hard it is being pressed onto the ground, we are often concerned about the location of the car's c.g., because that affects the contact forces at individual wheels. In the same way that one of two men carrying a deer hung from a pole will experience different weights if the deer is not centered on the pole, moving any of the separate weights that make up the car (thus changing the location of its c.g.) will affect the loads on some tires compared to others. The location of the c.g., then, has a critical effect on how a car goes, stops, and handles, and knowledge of the location of the c.g. is essential for many calculations concerned with acceleration, braking, and handling.

The first step in establishing the location of a car's c.g. is to measure the weight resting on each of the four wheels. Suppose we do this for some imaginary race car and come up with the following figures:

Left front	354 lb
Right front	256 lb
Left rear	650 lb
Right rear	470 lb
Total	1,730 lb

If we add the lefts, rights, fronts, and rears together, we come up with the following subtotals:

Left side   354 + 650 = 1,004
Right side   256 + 470 = 726
(As a check, note that the total *has to* equal 1,730 lb.)

Front   354 + 256 = 610
Rear   650 + 470 = 1,120
(Again, the total has to be 1,730 lb; it is.)

Next, we look at the fraction of the total weight of 1,730 pounds carried by each end and by each side:

Front $\frac{610}{1,730} \cong 0.35$, or 35%

Rear $\frac{1,120}{1,730} \cong 0.65$, or 65%

(In fact, because the front plus the rear has to equal the total, we could have determined that 65 percent of the weight is on the rear simply by subtracting the 35 percent that is on the front from 100 percent. Going through the exercise again, however, serves as a check; if the total doesn't equal 100 percent, we have goofed somewhere.)

Left side $\frac{1,004}{1,730} \cong 0.58$, or 58%

Right side $\frac{726}{1,730} \cong 0.42$, or 42%

These fractions or percentages tell us that the c.g. is located 65 percent of the wheelbase from the front (or 35 percent from the rear), and is 58 percent of the

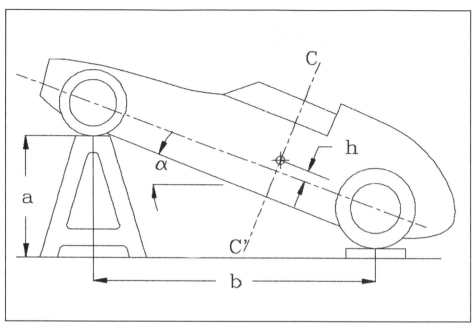

Figure 41: Determining the vertical location of a car's center of gravity is a bit trickier. One accepted method is to raise one end of the car and then measure the change in the wheel loading at the low end, followed by a little more math.

track width from the right side (or 42 percent from the left). Let us assume that the car has a wheelbase of 90 inches and a track width of 60 inches, then the c.g. lies $0.65 \times 90 = 58.5$ inches behind the front axle line, and $0.58 \times 60 = 34.8$ inches left of a line joining the front and rear tire centerlines (see figure 40).

The imaginary car in this example has its weight offset to the left, as is typical of left-turn-only racers. Road race and drag cars, on the other hand, are usually very close to symmetrical, so the above procedure can be simplified, using only the total front and rear axle weights to establish the front-to-rear location of the c.g., ignoring its side-to-side position on the assumption that it is at (or very near) the vehicle's centerline.

We have determined the location of the c.g. in two planes, so we know that it lies somewhere along the line C-C' in figure 41, but we still do not know where it is located in the vertical plane—how high off the ground it is. There are a handful of ways to do that, but one of the more straightforward is to raise one end of the vehicle, as illustrated in figure 41, and reweigh the load on the wheels remaining at ground level. Having measured the wheelbase and the angle of inclination, and knowing the longitudinal position of the c.g. from the above procedure, its vertical position can be reckoned as follows:

$$h = \frac{(W_{new} - W_{old})wb}{W_{total} \cdot \tan\alpha}$$

where: h = height of c.g. above the axle centerline, inches
W_{new} = weight on axle with car elevated, lb
W_{old} = weight on axle with car on ground, lb
wb = wheelbase, inches
W_{total} = total vehicle weight, lb
$\tan\alpha$ = tangent of angle of tilt

(But note that if the front and rear wheel and tire sizes are different, as in figure 41, then the value of h returned by the above equation is actually the height of the c.g. above a line joining the front and rear axle centerlines.)

On our imaginary car, wb = 90 inches, W_{total} = 1,730 lb, and W_{old} = 1,120 lb. Let's suppose W_{new} is 1,147 lb, and we measure the angle of tilt to be 22 degrees. Looking up the tangent of 22 degrees in a set of trig tables (or using a calculator that has a "tan" function) we discover $\tan\alpha$ = 0.4040. In fact, if we can measure dimensions a and b—see figure 4-12—with decent accuracy (note particularly that b is *not* the same as the wheelbase!), then we don't even need the trig tables or calculator, because $\tan\alpha = \frac{a}{b}$. In any case:

$$h = \frac{(W_{new} - W_{old})wb}{W_{total} \cdot \tan\alpha}$$

$$= \frac{(1{,}147 - 1{,}120) \times 90}{1{,}730 \times 0.4040}$$

$$= \frac{27 \times 90}{1{,}730 \times 0.4040}$$

$$\cong \frac{2{,}430}{698.9}$$

$$\cong 3.48$$

That is, the c.g. lies 3.48 inches above a line joining the axle centers. To make use of the position of the c.g. in further calculations (see chapter 5, Cornering Math), what we really need to know is the height of the c.g. above the ground, so we have to add the 3.48 inches to the distance from the ground to the line joining the axle centers. We could directly measure that distance (a taut piece of string could represent that invisible line), or we could work it out by trigonometry, or graphically (see the sidebar, "Back to the Drawing Board")

Chapter 5
Cornering
Math

I n chapter 3, Math of Acceleration and Braking, we defined acceleration (whether positive, as in a drag race, or negative, as when braking) as the rate of change of velocity. We also said there that, as long as the acceleration is taking place in a straight line, we could consider *velocity* to mean the same thing as *speed*, but that while speed is completely defined by just a number (e.g., 100 mph), velocity involves *both* speed *and* direction (e.g., 100 mph north). We promised there to further spell out this distinction; now seems as good a time as any, because cornering, even at a steady speed, involves acceleration.

Imagine you are facing directly north and a car approaches directly from the east. The driver of that car then turns toward the north (away from you) in a right-hand turn at a steady speed, continues through a complete U-turn, then drives off to the east again. When approaching, the car was moving from east to west; when leaving, it was moving from west to east. From your perspective, the car's speed in the east-to-west direction dwindled to zero (at the point when the car was aimed straight north), then "went negative" as it seemed (again from your point of view) to increase in speed eastbound, back to its original value, but in the opposite direction.

From your perspective, the car's apparent speed has undergone first a deceleration, then an acceleration. (It might help to imagine this all happening in the dark, so the only way you have of knowing the movement of the car is from a light on its roof.) From the driver's point of view, the speed has not changed. The key difference here is the frame of reference—the point of view. A physicist might say that speed refers to movement as seen from the moving car, while velocity refers to movement relative to a fixed observer—in this case, you.

No? That doesn't do it for you? Try this: consider the fuel in the tank of that car. If the car accelerated in a straight line, the fuel would slosh toward the back of the tank. That is because the fuel is being accelerated. You realize perfectly well that if the car turns left, the fuel will slosh to the right side of the tank. That too is because it is being accelerated. Why else?

94

Centrifugal Force

Any physicist will tell you that there is no such thing as "centrifugal force." I say: If you tie a large hex nut to a piece of string, and whirl the nut around over your head, you feel a pull in the string, and if that pull is not centrifugal force, then what is it? A physicist might say: Let's suppose that the string breaks at the very instant the nut, moving from your right to your left, passes directly in front of you. In that case, the nut will zip off in a straight line—*to your left*. Not straight away from you, mind, but to your left. The nut "wants" to go in a straight line, but the string applies a force that makes the nut steer constantly to the left; the pull you felt in the string is a reaction to the *centripetal acceleration* that the string applied to the nut. The fact that the nut does not fly straight out, radially, from the center of rotation (your hand) proves there is no force acting in that direction.

I say: Who cares? The pull in the string is real. Whether or not centrifugal force is a "phantom," whatever the trajectory of the nut if the string breaks, the pull the nut exerts on the string is unarguably in a radial direction. As long as the string remains unbroken, all we are interested in is the size of the pull in the string. There—I'm glad we cleared that up! In fact, whether

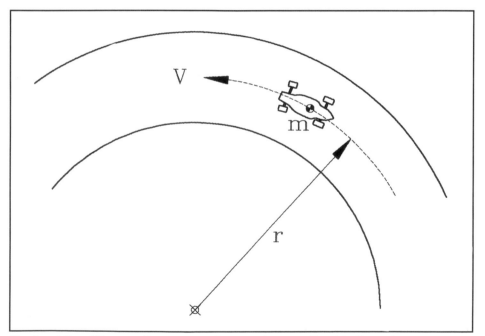

The "centrifugal" force acting on a car in a turn is proportional to the car's mass and the square of its speed, and is inversely proportional to the radius of the turn .

physicists wince or not, there is an equation for this nonexistent "centrifugal" force; here it is:

$$F_{cent} = \frac{m \cdot r \cdot n^2}{186.2}$$

where: F_{cent} = "centrifugal"(or centripetal) force, lb
              m = object mass, lb
              r = path radius, inches
              n = revolutions per minute

Let's suppose the nut in the above case weighs 1 ounce (0.0625 pound—I said it was a large nut!), the string is 24 inches long, and you were

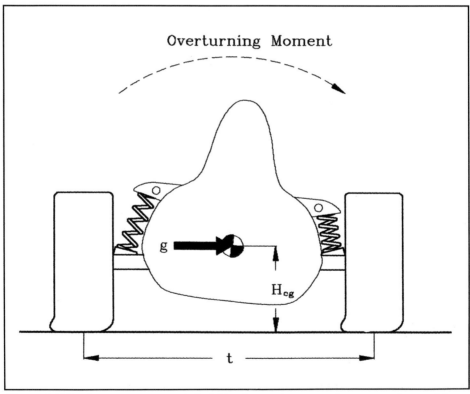

Figure 44: The torque, or moment, that tries to overturn a car in a corner is equal to the lateral acceleration in "g" multiplied by the height of the center of gravity. The total load transfer from inboard to outboard wheels, expressed as a fraction of the vehicle's mass, is that figure divided by the width of the track.

spinning it around your head once per second, that is, at 60 rpm. The force in the string will be:

$$F_{cent} = \frac{m \cdot r \cdot n^2}{186.2}$$

$$= \frac{0.0625 \times 24 \times 60^2}{186.2}$$

$$\cong 29 \text{ lb}$$

The equation as it stands is useful for figuring things like the force that tends to rip a fan's blades off its hub, or the force that makes the tire valve on a rotating road wheel tend to open, or that makes tire "bleeder" valves delay opening far beyond their "set" value. Indeed, these tire pressure relief valves used on many sprint cars simply cannot work as advertised, unless they are plumbed so that the valve itself lies right at the center of rotation of the wheel. Otherwise, the "nonexistent" centrifugal force will force the valve harder onto its seat. Working through the above equation using a representative figure of 0.9 grams (1.98 × 10^{-4} lb) for the weight of the movable valve parts, and a 15-inch wheel turning at 1,000 rpm, it has been demonstrated that a valve set to open at 10 psi will in fact have its opening delayed until the pressure reaches about 16 psi.

For other purposes, however, such as calculating how much a car is demanding of its tires in a corner, it is more convenient to work with vehicle speed in miles per hour, rather than its rate of driving around a circle in revolutions per minute, and to express the radius in feet, rather than inches. Reworked in this way, the equation becomes:

$$F_{cent} = \frac{m \cdot V^2}{14.97r}$$

where: F_{cent} = "centrifugal" (or centripetal) force, lb
m = vehicle mass, lb
V = vehicle velocity, mph
r = path radius, ft

For an example, let's look at a car weighing 1,850 pounds negotiating a turn with a radius of 840 feet while traveling at 110 mph.

$$F_{cent} = \frac{m \cdot V^2}{14.97r}$$

$$= \frac{1,850 \times 110^2}{14.97 \times 840}$$

$$\cong 1,780 \text{ lb}$$

Comparing the 1,780-pound force the tires have to develop to overcome the "centrifugal" force with the 1,850-pound normal force clamping them on the pavement, the vehicle is cornering at $\frac{1,780}{1,850} \cong 0.96$ g . (For an explanation of "normal force" and "g", see chapter 3, Math of Acceleration and Braking.)

Lateral Acceleration

That figure of 0.96 g in the above example is, in fact, the vehicle's *lateral acceleration*, expressed in units of "g". If that is all we are interested in, we do not need to know the weight of the car; all we need is the turn radius and the speed, as follows:

$$g_{lat} = \frac{V^2}{14.97r}$$

where: g_{lat} = lateral acceleration, g
V = velocity, mph
r = path radius, ft

(As explained in chapter 3, we can translate "g" into units of ft/sec² by multiplying by 32. Thus, the car in the previous example is accelerating at 0.96 × 32 ≅ 30.7 ft/sec².)

As a worked example of the above equation, let's pick a car running through a turn with a radius of 132 feet at a steady 50 mph.

$$g_{lat} = \frac{V^2}{14.97r}$$

$$= \frac{50^2}{14.97 \times 132}$$

$$\cong 1.27 \text{ g}$$

Weight Transfer from Cornering

Also in chapter 3, we discussed the load transfer toward the rear that takes place when a car is accelerated in a straight line, and toward the front when it is braked. Because cornering involves acceleration, there will also be a load transfer when cornering. This comes about because the force that shoves the car sideways toward the center of the turn originates at the point where the rubber meets the road—that is, at ground level—while the mass of the car all lies above ground level. The offset between the line of the force and the center of the mass it is working against produces a torque that tends to make the car overturn toward the outside of the corner.

We can calculate the size of this load transfer as follows:

$$\Delta_{load} = \frac{H_{cg} \cdot g}{t}(W_{tot})$$

where: Δ_{load} = load transfer, lb

H_{cg} = height of mass center, inches

g = acceleration, g

t = track, inches

W_{tot} = total vehicle weight, lb

(The symbol Δ is the Greek letter "delta." It is commonly used in mathematical expressions to stand for "difference" or "change in.")

Let's look again at the imaginary race car used in the example immediately above. We established that the vehicle is cornering at 1.27 g. Let's say it weighs 1,450 pounds, that the mass center is 17 inches above ground, and that the track width of the car (also sometimes called "tread"—the center-line-to-centerline distance between the left-side tires and the right-side ones) is 62 inches.

$$\Delta_{load} = \frac{H_{cg} \cdot g}{t}(W_{tot})$$

$$= \frac{17 \times 1.27}{62}(1,450)$$

$$\cong 505 \text{ lb}$$

In other words, 505 pounds will be unloaded off the inside pair of tires and the same amount added to the load carried by the right-side pair. Assuming the 1,450 pounds were initially shared equally between left and right sides—that is, there was no weight "bias," so there was 1,450 ÷ 2 = 725 lb on each side—then the inside pair (the left, on a left-turning car) will be carrying just 725 − 505 = 220 lb, while the outside pair will be burdened with 725 + 505 = 1,230 lb.

Wheel Loads When Cornering

Just because we know what the *total* load transfer is from the inside pair of wheels to the outside pair doesn't mean we know how that load transfer gets shared between front and rear. It may seem, on the face of it, that this fore-aft distribution of the load will simply be the same as the nominal front-rear weight distribution, but this will only be so if the front and rear suspension and springs are identical, which is almost never the case. In every other situation, one end or the other will do the lion's share of the work, and this phenomenon lies at the root of "chassis tuning." By varying spring rates and other factors, it is possible to totally alter the distribution of load at all four corners, and thus the handling of the car.

Expressed as simply as possible, a pair of tires gives the highest cornering power when a load is shared *equally* between the pair; any inequality in the loading will reduce the total cornering power of the pair. By forcing one end of the car to handle more than its share of the load transfer that inevitably occurs in cornering (say, by fitting stiffer springs there), the cornering power at that end will be reduced. Thus, a car that "pushes" (*understeers*) can have this tendency reduced by forcing the rear pair of tires to take more of the load transfer, and vice versa. (For much more detail on this somewhat complex yet subtle subject, see my book *Circle Track Suspension*, published by MBI Publishing Company.)

The first task is to establish the overall roll angle of the car, and to do that we need to get a handle on a concept called the *roll center*. If you view a photograph, taken from the front or rear, of a vehicle that is cornering hard, you can make out that the vehicle has rolled through a certain angle, and you can also estimate the center of that rolling movement—the point around which the vehicle seems to be rotating. You can achieve better accuracy in this

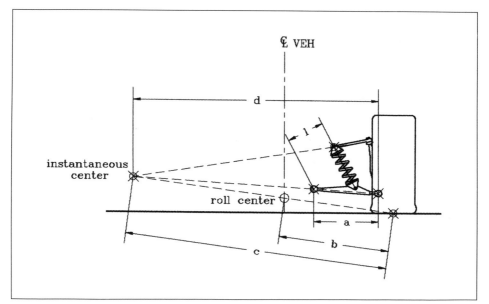

Figure 45: Sorting out *individual* wheel loads when cornering requires a knowledge of location of the roll center and of the instantaneous center of rotation of the suspension linkage at each end of the car.

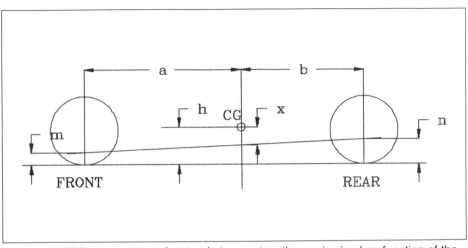

Figure 46: While the moment that tends to *overturn* the car is simply a function of the lateral acceleration and the center of gravity height, the *roll* moment depends on the lateral acceleration and the height of the center of gravity above the roll axis, here the dimension *x* .

estimate if you work with a scale drawing of the suspension system, such as the figure 45.

With the "wishbone" type suspension illustrated there, the point marked as "instantaneous center" lies at the point where the lines of the upper and lower suspension links converge. That point shifts about as the suspension moves, of course, but at any instant (hence the name) this is the center that the wheel moves around—it is as if the wheel's movement is guided by a simple swinging axle hinged at that point. It is the contact patch of the tire we are interested in, however, not the hub, so a third line is drawn back from the instantaneous center to the intersection of the tire and the ground. The roll center is found where that line crosses the vehicle centerline. Of course, there is a roll center for the suspension at the other end of the car, and a line joining the two roll centers is the *axis* line that the car rolls around (it cannot roll around a *point*).

The centrifugal force that arises when the vehicle drives around a turn acts at the mass center (center of gravity), so a *roll moment*, or torque, is produced equal to the size of the centrifugal force multiplied by the vertical height from the c.g. to the roll axis, indicated in figure 46 as *x*. Mathematically:

$$M_{roll} = m \cdot x \cdot g$$

where: M_{roll} = roll moment, in-lb
m = vehicle mass, lb
x = vertical height from c.g to roll axis
g = lateral acceleration, g

The springs resist this rolling by generating a *restoring moment* in the opposite direction. Thinking first about the front suspension, as the car rolls the compression of the spring on one side and the extension of the spring on the other side will produce a restoring moment of:

$$M_{resf} = 2k_s\alpha\frac{l^2d^2b}{57.3a^2c^2}$$

where: M_{resf} = restoring moment from front springs, in-lb
  k_s = rate of *one* front spring, lb/in
  α = roll angle, degrees
  l, a, b, c, d as indicated in the illustration

In chapter 4, Chassis Math, we showed how to arrive at the spring rate measured at the wheel—the wheel rate, k_w—given the rate at the spring, k_s, and the dimensions of the suspension components. If you have already done that, then the equation simplifies to:

$$M_{resf} = 2k_w\alpha\frac{b}{57.3}$$

Likewise, the rear springs will produce a restoring moment, M_{resr}, figured in exactly the same way. Together, they will produce a total restoring moment $M_{rest} = M_{resf} + M_{resr}$. The final roll angle represents the position at which the restoring moment exactly matches the roll moment. In other words, when $M_{rest} = M_{roll}$. That is, when:

$$m \cdot x \cdot g = 2k\alpha\frac{b}{57.3}[\text{front}] + 2k\alpha\frac{b}{57.3}[\text{rear}]$$

In any real world case, all the numerical values will be known, except for α, so by substituting those numbers into the equation and transposing, the value of α will emerge.

Note that the vehicle as a whole can only roll through one single angle (assuming the chassis is stiff—and that is why chassis stiffness is important), so the value of α will be the same at both ends. By plugging this value back into the equation, the restoring moment there, and thus the load transfer, can be calculated (note that we couldn't do this before, because we didn't know what α was), and the same procedure applied to the rear.

The above is surely the toughest math in this book, but even so a lot of simplifying assumptions have been made. No account has been taken, for

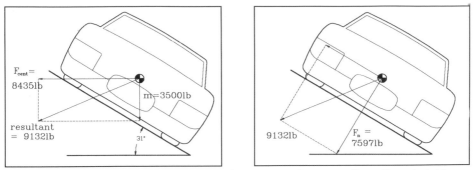

Whether a turn is banked or flat, the only forces at work are gravity, acting straight downward, and centrifugal force, acting horizontally. The resultant of these two can be determined graphically, as shown (*Figure 47*, left). With that resultant established, it can be transposed to a new frame of reference aligned with the track (*Figure 48*, right). Now both the normal force and the force tending to slide the car up the banking can also be plotted.

instance, of the *unsprung* mass—the wheels, tires, brakes, etc. . . . everything that bounces up and down relative to the chassis—and these parts also have roll moments of their own. Not only does the car try to fall over on its side, so does each wheel, etc. We have also ignored the contribution of any anti-roll bar(s). Also, the idea that the roll center is on the vehicle centerline is only partly valid—there is considerable academic dispute about this matter. Still, the principles are basically sound. In the interests of space (and the author's sanity!) no example has been worked through. If you are feeling strong, you might care to work out your own.

Effects of Track Banking Angle

Another way to redistribute the load carried by left- and right-side pairs of tires is to tilt the surface the vehicle is on. Now, there is obviously some critical angle of tilt beyond which the vehicle will simply tip over on its side—that is, all of the load is on the "downhill" side; 100 percent of the load previously carried by the "uphill" pair of tires has been transferred. Yet when the vehicle is on flat ground, the left- and right-side pairs of tires will each experience the same normal force, assuming the vehicle is symmetrical. (Indeed, that is essentially what we mean by "symmetrical.") Between these two limits, then, the size of the load shift evidently depends on the angle of tilt.

One of the effects of banked turns on the race track, then, is to provide a countervail to the load transfer in the opposite direction of what occurs when cornering, as described above. At some particular speed, these two effects will perfectly cancel each other. When the Indianapolis race track was first planned, for example, the 9-degree bank angle of its 840-foot-radius turns was designed to achieve this equilibrium at 60 mph—at that speed, the car could be driven "hands off."

Another effect of banked turns, however, is to increase the normal force of *all* the tires. To explain, the centrifugal force of a vehicle cornering in a banked turn continues to act horizontally, but because the surface is slanted, part of that force acts at right angles to the track surface, tending to push the car harder onto the pavement, while the other part acts to push the car "uphill."

Once the centrifugal force has been calculated based on speed and turn radius, as detailed above, one way to determine the actual numerical values of the tire loads is by graphical methods, as described in chapter 4, Chassis Math. The results of such an exercise are shown in the adjacent illustration, assuming a 3,500-pound car traveling 190 mph in a 1,000-foot-radius turn with a 31-degree bank angle. (These approximately correspond to the values for a Winston Cup car on the Daytona banking.)

The reckoning can also be done by straight mathematical calculation using trigonometry. First, we compute the lateral acceleration, using the equation:

$$g_{lat} = \frac{V^2}{14.97r}$$

$$= \frac{190^2}{14.97 \cdot 1,000}$$

$$\cong 2.41 \text{ g}$$

Given that, the equation for the normal force is:

$$F_n = m(g \sin \alpha + \cos \alpha)$$

where: F_n = normal force, lb
m = vehicle mass, lb
g = lateral acceleration, g
α = angle of bank from horizontal

Thus, for our example:

$$F_n = m(g \sin \alpha + \cos \alpha)$$

$$= 3,500(2.41 \sin 31 + \cos 31)$$

$$\cong 3,500(2.41 \cdot 0.545 + 0.857)$$

$$\cong 7,597 \text{ lb}$$

If you regarded the 2.41 g arrived at above as an improbably high figure, the explanation just emerged: the car is being clamped onto the track with a force $\frac{7,597}{3,500} \cong 2.17$ times the vehicle mass; to achieve a lateral acceleration of 2.41 g, the tires only have to have a value of $\mu = \frac{2.41}{2.17} \cong 1.1$, a completely believable value for a race tire.

104

Chapter 6

Math of Fluids and Flows

Density/Specific Gravity

The *density* of a substance is an expression of how much a certain volume of it weighs, expressed as units of weight per unit of volume. In the British system of measurements, the units are usually pounds per cubic inch (lb/in^3) or pounds per cubic foot (lb/ft^3). As the "/" suggests, the actual numerical value of a substance's density is a matter of weighing a sample of it, then dividing that weight by the volume of the sample.

For example, we have a cylindrical slug of some sort of metal, although we may not know what metal it is at this point, that measures 2.25 inches in diameter (i.e., 1.125-inch radius) and is 4.75 inches long. We set it on a scale and determine that it weighs 1.9 pounds. Next, we have to calculate its volume. (It should be obvious that the volume of a cylinder is the same whether the cylinder is a solid lump of something or an empty space; it is the size of the space that we are interested in.) We provided the equation for calculating the volume of a cylinder in chapter 2, Engine and Power Math, as follows:

$$V = \pi r^2 h$$

where: V = cylinder volume, ci
          r = radius of the cylinder, inches
          h = height (or length) of the cylinder, inches

So: $V = \pi \cdot 1.125^2 \cdot 4.75$

$\cong 18.9$ ci

Since it weighs 1.9 pounds, the density is $1.9 \div 18.9 \cong 0.1\ lb/in^3$. Table 6A lists the densities of a number of common materials. From that table, we can readily see that this chunk of metal must be aluminum. (Note that it hardly matters what alloy of aluminum we are dealing with; all of the very wide range of alloys available fall between $0.093\ lb/in^3$ and $0.106\ lb/in^3$.)

Table 2
Density and Specific Gravity of Some Common Substances

	Density (lb/in³)	Specific Gravity
Water	0.036	1.0
Granite	0.09	2.7
Cast iron	0.25–0.28	7.1–7.7
Steel	0.28–0.30	7.7–8.3
Aluminum	0.09–0.10	2.5–2.8
Magnesium	0.06–0.065	1.7–1.8
Titanium	0.162–0.166	4.5–4.6
Spruce wood	0.016–0.019	0.44–0.52
Fiberglass/epoxy	0.062–0.072	1.72–1.99
Carbon fiber/epoxy	0.056–0.061	1.55–1.69

The *specific gravity* (s.g.) of a substance is a measure of how its density compares with that of water. Pure water weighs 0.03613 lb/in³, or 62.43 lb/ft³, and this is defined as an s.g. of 1. Table 6A, which lists the densities of some materials, also lists their s.g. Inspection of that table confirms what should be obvious from the above: the s.g. of a substance is its density divided by 0.03613.

It is worth mentioning here that this issue of density versus s.g. is much simpler when working in the metric system. There, the s.g. of water is still defined as 1, but density is measured in grams-per-cubic centimeter (gm/cc) and, because the gram was essentially defined that way, 1 cubic centimeter of water weighs 1 gram. Thus, in the metric system, the s.g. of a substance is exactly the same as its density in gm/cc.

Effects of Temperature and Pressure (The Gas Laws)

Generally speaking, you cannot put a quart into a pint container—but you can when you are dealing with a gas. Unlike liquid or solid substances, the molecules in gases can fairly readily be spread further apart (*rarefied*), or squeezed closer together (*compressed*), so a certain fixed quantity of gas, by weight, can occupy just about any volume you would like.

If you do squeeze a "quart" of gas into a pint container, you will discover that the pressure of the gas rises. If the "quart" of gas you are working with is air from the atmosphere that you just trapped in a can (by putting a lid on it), then the gas started off at the pressure of the atmosphere, which is about 14.7 psi on a "standard" day. If you then stuffed that same quantity of gas into a pint container (be quick with the lid!), a gauge connected to the pint container would show a pressure of 29.4 psi—exactly twice what we started with.

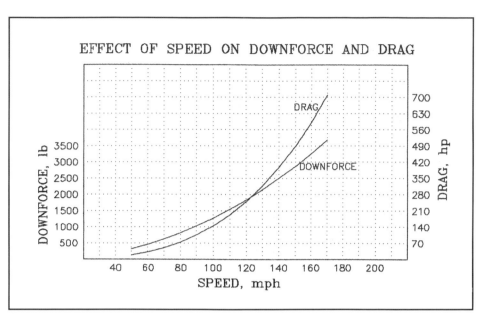

Figure 49: An ideal demonstration of the difference between a "square law" function and a "cube law" function (see also chapter 1) is the relationship between the price to be paid in horsepower for a given amount of downforce from a wing. The downforce varies with speed *squared*, while the power consumed by drag increases with speed *cubed*.

At this point we should explain that the pressure gauge in this case must be one that measures *absolute* pressure. Most automotive type pressure gauges show zero when they are just sitting on a workbench, not hooked up to anything. But it is important to understand that the zero mark on the dial is, in a sense, offset by 14.7 psi. The gauge (and you, and everything else on the surface of the earth) is operating at a pressure of 14.7 psi above an absolute vacuum. Some pressure gauges *do* read in absolute pressure. We can distinguish between the two by use of the terms *psia* (psi, absolute) and *psig* (psi, gauge).

We touched on this issue of the connection between the pressure and the volume of a gas when discussing gas springs in chapter 4, Chassis Math. There, we labeled this relationship as Boyle's law. Expressed mathematically:

$$P \cdot V = k$$

where: P = the pressure (any units)
           V = the volume (any units)
           k = a constant number (varies with the units)

Expressed in words, Boyle's law says that if the temperature is kept constant, the pressure of a fixed mass of gas varies directly according to the volume of its container—the pressure times the volume is always some constant number.

An example: one cylinder of an engine having a compression ratio of 9:1 is filled with a mixture of air and gasoline vapor (which is also a gas) at atmospheric pressure, then the piston rises to the top of the cylinder. What is the pressure in the cylinder at TDC?

$$P \cdot V = k$$

$$\therefore \quad P_1 \cdot V_1 = P_2 \cdot V_2$$

where: P_1 = pressure at BDC
                  V_1 = volume at BDC
                  P_2 = pressure at TDC
                  V_2 = volume at TDC

$$\therefore \quad P_2 = \frac{P_1 \cdot V_1}{V_2}$$

i.e., $P_2 = P_1 \left(\dfrac{V_1}{V_2} \right)$

Note that we do not have to know the values of V_1 or V_2; it is the *ratio* of the two that affects things, and we know that to be $\frac{9}{1} = 9$, so:

$$P_2 = 14.7 \times 9$$

$$= 132.3 \text{ psi}$$

Boyle's law is half of what are termed the *gas laws*; the other half is provided by Charles' law. Jacques Charles (1746–1823) was a French academic involved, among other things, in the earliest days of balloon flight. Building on Boyle's observations about the relationship between the volume and the pressure of a fixed quantity of gas, Charles examined the effects of *temperature* changes, and discovered that, if the pressure is kept constant, the volume of a fixed mass of gas varies directly with its absolute temperature.

Ahh, there is that word *absolute* again. To explain, just as we may be misled when dealing with pressures by the placement of the zero marks on our pressure gauges, so we may be led astray by the placement of the zero marks on our thermometers. Anyone who lives in the northern half of the continent is well aware that it is possible for things to get colder than zero on anybody's temperature scale, so just how cold can things get? The answer was provided by Lord Kelvin: -459.4 degrees Fahrenheit, or -273 degrees Celsius. At that temperature, all molecular motion ceases. Kelvin termed this "absolute zero," and the temperature scale he invented is called the "absolute scale," or the "Kelvin scale." To convert any temperature in degrees Fahrenheit to degrees Kelvin (degK), just add 459.4.

So, back to Charles' law. Expressed mathematically:

$$\frac{t}{V} = k$$

where: t = temperature, degK
V = the volume (any units)
k = a constant number (varies with the units)

So, if we heat a certain quantity of gas from some initial temperature, t_1, to some higher temperature, t_2, and allow the gas to expand without confining it (that is, we do not allow its pressure to rise), then its volume after the heating, V_2, will be given by:

$$V_2 \cdot t_1 = V_1 \cdot t_2$$

$$V_2 = \frac{V_1 \cdot t_2}{t_1}$$

i.e., $V_2 = V_1\left(\dfrac{t_2}{t_1}\right)$

As an example, let's calculate the increase in the volume of any fixed quantity (mass) of air drawn from the engine compartment of a 1970 Camaro driving at 70 mph on a 70°F day, where the underhood air temperature is 170°F. (These are actual figures from a test conducted by GM.)

$$V_2 = V_1\left(\frac{t_2}{t_1}\right)$$

$$= V_1\left(\frac{170 + 459.4}{70 + 459.4}\right) \quad \text{(add 459.4 to change °F to degK)}$$

$$= V_1\left(\frac{629.4}{529.4}\right)$$

$$\cong 1.19V_1$$

Thus, the air will occupy about 19 percent more volume, but since we are talking about a fixed mass, its density will drop correspondingly. The new density will be just $\frac{1}{1.19} \cong 0.84$ as great as before heating, so the mass of air in a given "lung-full" inhaled by the engine will be 16 percent less ($1 - 0.84 = 0.16$) than if the engine were breathing outside air. Because the power of an engine is a function of the mass of air handled per minute, then at the same engine spced the power will likewise be reduced by 16 percent.

When changes in both temperature and pressure are encountered, Boyle's law and Charles's law can be combined to give:

$$\frac{P \cdot V}{t} = k$$

If P_1, V_1, and t_1 respectively represent the pressure, volume, and absolute temperature under one set of conditions, and P_2, V_2, and t_2 the same variables under another set of conditions, then the following relationship is also true:

$$\frac{P_1 \cdot V_1}{t_1} = \frac{P_2 \cdot V_2}{t_2}$$

Gas Velocity Through Pipes/Ports

Suppose we have a fairly free-breathing 350-ci V-8 engine running at wide open throttle (WOT) at 6,500 rpm, and that engine has a carburetor with four identical venturis, each of $1\frac{11}{16}$ inch diameter. What is the gas velocity through each venturi?

First we have to calculate the total volume of air flowing. A four-stroke engine theoretically inhales a volume of air equal to half its displacement, in this case 175 ci, with every revolution. Our hypothetical engine is turning 6,500 rpm, so that 175 ci will be breathed 6,500 times a minute. Because of friction losses in the piping, the *volumetric efficiency* (see chapter 2, Engine and Power Math) will be less than 100 percent; let's say 85 percent. So the total flow into the engine will be: $175 \times 6,500 \times 0.85 = 966,875$ cu in/min $\cong 560$ cu ft/min (1 cu ft = 1,728 cu in).

Each venturi handles only one-quarter the total, so the flow through one venturi will be $\frac{560}{4} = 140$cu ft/min (or 140 cfm).

Next we calculate the cross-sectional area of the venturi. $1\frac{11}{16} \cong 1.69$, so the area, A, is:

$$A = 0.7854D$$

$$= 0.7854 \times 1.69$$

$$\cong 1.327 \text{ sq in} \cong 0.0092 \text{ sq ft} \quad (1 \text{ sq ft} = 144 \text{ sq in})$$

Most folks have no problem up to this point, but stumble when actually trying to calculate the velocity of flow based on this information. Here's one way to think about it: A cylindrical "slug" of air with a volume of 140 cu ft and a cross-sectional area of 0.0092 sq ft passes through the hole every minute. All we have to do is figure out how *long* that "slug" is.

The volume of a cylinder, V, is its cross-sectional area, A, multiplied by its length (or height), h, so:

$$V = A \cdot h$$

$$h = \frac{V}{A}$$

$$= \frac{140}{0.0092}$$

$$\cong 15{,}217 \text{ ft (the length of the slug)}$$

So, the rate of flow is 15,217 ft/min, which is 253 ft/sec, which is about 173 mph.

Acoustic Ramming

The flow of gases through an engine is not smooth and continuous. Rather, it pulsates as the valves open and close. As each intake valve snaps open, for instance, the column of gas in the intake port is suddenly exposed to the reduced pressure in the cylinder caused by the rapidly descending piston. This creates a pulse of low pressure that travels back "upstream," toward the air inlet. Note that this pulse travels quite literally at the speed of sound, and completely independent of the bulk movement of those gases, so that pulse will reach the open end of the intake pipe even though the column of gas itself has barely begun to move.

It is a bit like tossing a pebble in a pond—ripples spread out from the point of impact toward the edges of the pond, then reflect back toward the center, yet there is no bulk movement of the water. A leaf floating on the surface, for example, will not be carried toward the edge, but will simply bob up and down as the peaks and hollows of the waves pass by.

Once that pulse of reduced pressure reaches fresh air, the surrounding atmosphere rushes in to fill the "hole," so a second pulse now reflects back toward the valve, except this time the pulse is one of *high* pressure. In turn, that reflected pulse zips downstream, toward the cylinder.

Upon reaching the end, another reflection occurs, but because that end of the pipe is closed (by the top of the piston), this time the reflected pulse has the same "sign" as the one that arrived—it is a high pressure or "positive" pulse. Now we have a positive pulse rushing toward the open end where it will be reflected as a negative one, and so on. Naturally, some energy is lost with every trip up and down the pipe, so the pressure pulses grow gradually weaker with every trip. In the meantime, good use can be made of the reflected high pressure pulses arriving at the cylinder.

If we can get the timing right, we can arrange for the intake valve to close just after the arrival of one of these high pressure pulses. Because the molecules are squeezed more lightly together within that positive pulse, a little more fuel/air mixture will wind up trapped inside the cylinder than would otherwise be the case. By this means, the VE of an engine can be raised a few percent, for a total that, in some cases, exceeds 100 percent. Free lunch!

Well, not quite. Recall that all these pressure waves are traveling at the speed of sound. (The speed of sound in a gasoline/air mixture at, say, 100°F is about 1,100 feet per second [fps].) The time for a single trip through the intake system, then, is established just by that speed and by the length of the pipe. Accordingly, this acoustic ramming effect will be experienced only at one specific engine speed. At other speeds, the pressure waves will be out of synch with the opening and closing of the valves, so the pressure in the cylinders may be (indeed, probably is) *lower* than otherwise. What helps at one particular rpm hurts at all others, so engines that take advantage of this technique are notoriously "peaky." Still, if the engine speed range can be kept within narrow bounds with close-ratio gears, the benefits can outweigh the drawbacks. The only remaining issue is to "tune" the length of pipe for whatever rpm is selected.

In general: $$L = \frac{K \cdot C}{N}$$

where: L = length of pipe, inches
K = a constant (see detail, below)
C = velocity of sound (approximately 1,100 fps)
N = rpm

Several researchers have investigated this effect; each seems to come up with a somewhat different value for K, partly no doubt because (as you may have figured out) the ideal moment to "trap" the available pulse also depends on the particular cam timing involved. Author Philip Smith, in *Scientific Design of Exhaust and Intake Systems,* quotes a value of $K = 90$. Chrysler engineers working on the "cross ram" manifold used on some of their high performance V-8s in the 1960s established a value of $K = 72$. Chrysler also implicitly acknowledged some degree of fuzziness in their calculations, providing a ±3-inch range of variability. Using Chrysler's numbers, and assuming a chosen speed of 4,000 rpm:

$$L = \frac{72 \times 1,100}{4,000} \pm 3$$

$$= 19.8 \pm 3 \text{ (i.e., 16.8–22.8 inches)}$$

Aerodynamic Drag

One of Newton's laws of motion asserts that a body in motion will continue in a straight line at constant speed unless acted upon by an external force. Everyday experience seems to contradict this—straight line, maybe; constant speed, no way. A car with the power shut off will definitely not continue at a constant speed; it will gradually coast to a halt. Yet Newton was right; the reason the car slows is because there *is* an external force acting—a friction force that arises partly from the flexing of the tires, the churning of oil in the transmission, and a host of other minor causes, but mostly from aerodynamic drag.

This force has two principal causes. The first results from the air molecules immediately adjacent to the body surface tending to "stick" to that surface and so getting carried along with it, while molecules further away from the body flow past at "free stream" speed. The scrubbing of the slow-moving molecules against the faster moving ones causes *skin friction*. Skin friction is significant for aircraft and Land Speed Record "streamliners," but is only a minor component in the aerodynamic drag of passenger or race car shapes at their typical speeds.

By far the largest source of air drag on unstreamlined car shapes arises from pressure differences between the forward-facing and rearward-facing surfaces of the vehicle. Because of the comparatively clumsy shape (what aerodynamicists call a *bluff body*), air piles up in front—raising the pressure there—and is unable to close in smoothly at the back, causing a drop in the prevailing pressure at the rear of the car. The net effect of this push on the front and pull on the back is termed *form* (shape) *drag*.

The aerodynamic force attributable to the form drag, expressed in pounds, is given by:

$$F_{drag} \cong \frac{C_d \cdot A \cdot V^2}{400}$$

where: F_{drag} = aerodynamic drag, lb
C_d = drag coefficient (no units)
A = frontal area, sq ft
V = velocity, mph

We should explain some of these terms. The drag coefficient, C_d, is simply a number (with no units attached) that compares the "slipperiness" of a shape to that of a flat plate square on to the airstream. That "barn door" reference figure is taken to be 1.2; a typical modern sedan has a C_d of 0.35–0.45; a perfect "streamlined" teardrop shape might have a C_d as low as 0.03.

The frontal area, A, is simply the size of the car (or other object) viewed head-on from the front. While there are various methods for assessing a car's frontal area, ranging from tracing a photo onto graph paper and counting squares, through very precise laser "planimetry," a rough ballpark figure for any conventional automobile is 80 percent of the height times the width.

Let's take as an example a vehicle with a C_d of 0.44 and a frontal area, A, of 19.25 square feet (which, by the way, happen to be the relevant figures for a VW Beetle) running at 55 mph:

$$F_{drag} \cong \frac{C_d \cdot A \cdot V^2}{400}$$

$$\cong \frac{0.44 \times 19.25 \times 55^2}{400}$$

$$\cong 64 \text{ lb}$$

It is often more convenient to think of drag in terms of horsepower, rather than a certain number of pounds. The equation for calculating aerodynamic drag expressed as horsepower is given by:

$$Drag_{hp} \cong \frac{C_d \cdot A \cdot V^3}{15 \times 10^4}$$

where: $Drag_{hp}$ = aerodynamic drag, horsepower
C_d = drag coefficient (no units)
A = frontal area, sq ft
V = velocity, mph

We'll rework the VW Beetle example, using this equation:

$$Drag_{hp} \cong \frac{C_d \cdot A \cdot V^3}{15 \times 10^4}$$

$$\cong \frac{0.44 \times 19.25 \times 55^3}{15 \times 10^4}$$

$$\cong 9.4 \text{ hp}$$

This may seem too low, but remember that this ignores the contribution of tire drag. In truth, the real power consumption of a car running on flat ground at a modest constant speed is remarkably low. But look what happens when we increase the speed. We will pick 72 mph, because that is pretty close to the top speed of an old Beetle.

$$Drag_{hp} \cong \frac{C_d \cdot A \cdot V^3}{15 \times 10^4}$$

$$\cong \frac{0.44 \times 19.25 \times 72^3}{15 \times 10^4}$$

$$\cong 21 \text{ hp}$$

While the fact that the drag horsepower has more than doubled for just a 30 percent increase in speed drives home the point that drag horsepower varies as the *cube* of the speed (V^3), the total again seems low, but recall that we have not taken tire drag into account, which is known to be about 4–5 horsepower at that speed. We also happen to know that, while the power output of an early VW engine was 36 horsepower, measured *at the flywheel*, only 31–32 horsepower made it to the rear wheels. So, total drag at 72 mph is at least 25 horsepower, while there is 31–32 horsepower available. With just 5 or so horsepower left over, and thus available to accelerate the car, it is easy to see why these old hair dryers just ran out of steam at a bit over 70 mph.

We can take another opportunity to practice transposing terms by using the drag equation to calculate the theoretical top speed of a car when the horsepower, C_d, and A are known. Let's consider something that has about 21 square feet of frontal area, a C_d of about 0.31, and maybe 700 horsepower, figures typical of a Winston Cup car of a handful of years back.

$$Drag_{hp} \cong \frac{C_d \cdot A \cdot V^3}{15 \times 10^4}$$

$$700 = \frac{0.31 \times 21 \times V^3}{15 \times 10^4} \quad \text{(set } Drag_{hp} = \text{ known power)}$$

$$700 \times 15 \times 10^4 = 0.31 \times 21 \times V^3 \text{ (multiply both sides by } 15 \times 10^4 \text{)}$$

$$0.31 \times 21 \times V^3 = 700 \times 15 \times 10^4$$
$$\text{(swap sides, to get } V^3 \text{ on the left)}$$

$$V^3 = \frac{700 \times 15 \times 10^4}{0.31 \times 21} \quad \text{(divide both sides by } 0.31 \times 21 \text{)}$$

$$V^3 \cong 16{,}129{,}032 \text{ (do the arithmetic)}$$

$$V \cong \sqrt[3]{16{,}129{,}032}$$

$$\cong 253 \text{ mph}$$

Aerodynamic Lift/Downforce

Whether you regard it as a good thing or not, you have to admit that the introduction of inverted wings on race cars is one of the most significant events in the history of motor sports. By pressing the tires more firmly onto the road, wings dramatically increase the vehicle's traction capability, which permits much faster cornering, shorter braking distances, and in some cases, reduces or eliminates wheelspin when accelerating, especially at high speeds.

Needless to say, the "lift" forces from wings have been studied for decades by the aircraft industry. (Although it is a bit contradictory, the force of a wing in the vertical direction is called *lift* whether it acts up or down.) The properties of literally thousands of different wing shapes, or *profiles*, have been tested and catalogued, and the basic equation for lift was developed when your granddad was a boy. It is:

$$F_{lift} = 0.00256 \cdot C_l \cdot S \cdot V^2$$

where: F_{lift} = lift force, lb
C_l = lift coefficient (no units)
S = airfoil area, sq ft
V = velocity, mph

The lift coefficient, C_l, has a meaning analogous to C_d: it is a "dimensionless" coefficient (there are no units attached) that expresses the efficiency of one shape at producing lift, relative to another. The value of any wing's C_l varies according to the angle at which it encounters the air stream, called the *angle of attack*, or *angle of incidence*. For any given profile, the C_l increases pretty much linearly with the angle of attack, up to some maximum point at which the wing "stalls"—further increases in the angle of attack lead to less lift, not more.

The profiles used on most aircraft wings have a maximum C_l of maybe 1.5–1.6; some recent very high performance shapes achieve 2.0 or better. But when multiple wing elements are stacked together to create the "Venetian blind" arrangements seen on many modern race cars, the overall C_l of such a "cascade" can reach 3.5 or more.

Another point that needs clarification is that the wing area, A, is reckoned differently from the frontal area of a car. The area of a wing is based on its *plan* area—the area you see when you view directly from above.

As an example, let's look at a "single element" wing (no "cascade" of multiple sections) typical of the type fitted to a small open wheel road racer. The side-to-side dimension, or *span*, of such a wing might be around 50 inches, while the front-to-back dimension, or *chord*, might be 14 inches. The plan area, then, is $\frac{50 \times 14}{144} \cong 4.86$ sq ft. (We divided by 144 to convert square inches into square feet.) We'll pick a value of C_l of 1.5, representative of a single-element wing, and assume a speed of 100 mph.

$$F_{lift} = 0.00256 \cdot C_l \cdot S \cdot V^2$$

$$= 0.00256 \times 1.5 \times 4.86 \times 100^2$$

$$\cong 187 \text{ lb}$$

As usual, of course, there is no such thing as a free lunch, and the downward-acting force provided by a wing comes with a price attached— additional aerodynamic drag. This "price paid for lift" is termed *induced* drag, and is calculated by the following:

$$Drag_i = 24.37 \cdot 10^{-5} \left(\frac{C_l^2}{\pi \cdot AR} \right) S \cdot V^2$$

where: $Drag_i$ = induced drag due to lift, lb
  C_l = lift coefficient (no units)
  AR = aspect ratio = $\frac{span^2}{S}$ (no units)
  S = airfoil area, sq ft
  V = velocity, mph

The only additional term in here that may require some clarification is the *aspect ratio*, AR. If the shape of the wing is perfectly rectangular in plan view, then the AR is simply the span divided by the chord. Because many wings are either tapered or otherwise vary in chord at different positions along the span (especially on aircraft, but also the front wings on many race cars), AR is expressed as $\frac{span^2}{S}$, where S is the wing area, as figured above. For the wing on our imaginary small road racer, the span is $50 \div 12 = 4.17$ ft, while $S = 4.86$ sq ft, so $AR = \frac{4.17^2}{4.86} \cong 3.58$.

$$Drag_i = 24.37 \cdot 10^{-5} \left(\frac{C_l^2}{\pi \cdot AR} \right) S \cdot V^2$$

$$= 24.37 \cdot 10^{-5} \left(\frac{1.5^2}{\pi \cdot 3.58} \right) 4.86 \cdot 100^2$$

$$\cong 24.37 \cdot 10^{-5} \left(\frac{2.25}{11.25} \right) 4.86 \cdot 10^4 \qquad (100^2 = 10^4)$$

$$\cong 24.37(0.2)4.86 \cdot 10^{-1} \qquad (10^{-5} \times 10^4 = 10^{-1})$$

$$\cong 2.37 \text{ lb}$$

Note in the above that if the value of C_l is zero, then the whole right side of the equation equals zero, that is, $Drag_i = 0$. In other words, if a wing is not producing any lift, then it is not producing any induced drag either. But that is not to say that such a wing does not create *any* drag; even though it is a highly streamlined shape, there must still be *some* drag, arising simply from a combination of skin friction and form drag.

As with the form drag of a bluff body, the drag from this source is a function of speed, area, and a drag coefficient, C_d. As you might expect, the C_d varies from one profile to another; as you might *not* expect, it also depends on the C_l at which the wing is operating. The same tables of wing sections that set out the C_l in relation to the angle of attack also list the C_d; for our race car wing we will pick a typical value of $C_d = 0.02$ at a C_l of 1.5. (Note that the area, A, is again based on the plan area.)

The equation for this "basic" drag is:

$$D = 24.37 \cdot 10^{-5} \cdot C_d \cdot S \cdot V^2$$

For our example, then:

$$D = 24.37 \cdot 10^{-5} \cdot 0.02 \cdot 4.86 \cdot 100^2$$

$$\cong 0.24 \text{ lb}$$

On race cars, the basic form and skin drag are negligible, compared to the induced drag, because of their tiny values of AR; on aircraft, where large spans yield large values of AR, the situation is very much the other way around.

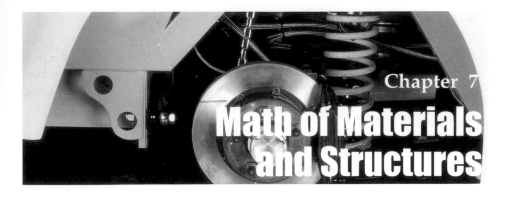

Chapter 7

Math of Materials and Structures

Strength of Materials

Everybody knows from everyday experience that steel is stronger than, say, wood. And that wood is stronger than linoleum. But when they try to get much further in understanding the subject generally termed "the strength of materials," most people get thoroughly hung up. Part of the reason for this, I suspect, is the huge spread between the strengths of common materials. While you can easily break a linoleum tile with your bare hands and while, with some effort, you can snap a broomstick over your knee, you cannot do the same with a crowbar. Here, everyday experience seems to tell us that the crowbar is "unbreakable." So, let's get one thing straight from the start: *Everything* breaks if you apply enough force to it.

I believe another reason people's brows get wrinkled when dealing with this subject is the terminology used. Words like *stress* and *strain* and *strong* and *stiff* have rather special meanings to scientists and engineers working in the field of strength of materials, and while these specific definitions sometimes correspond to their everyday meanings, often they do not. This surely causes confusion and frustration. It is worth making an effort to understand the technical meanings of these terms, as explained below.

Finally, perhaps the greatest source of bafflement arises over the related concepts of *strain* and *stiffness*. Although everyday experience contradicts the idea, the simplest statement explaining the underlying concept has been attributed to Sir Henry Royce (of Rolls Royce fame) who said, "every engineering material is rubber." In other words, whenever you pull or push on something, whatever it might be made out of, it will stretch or grow shorter. And whenever you try to bend or twist something, you succeed. "Nah!" you say? Read on.

Stress

Imagine something long and straight—a piece of rope, a length of lumber, a steel rod. Now, firmly anchor one end and pull on the other. Let's say you pull with a force of 100 pounds, and let's say the rope, or lumber, or steel rod measures 1 inch by 1 inch. (I know, square ropes are hard to find! If you are thinking rope, then imagine that it is a bit more than $1\frac{1}{8}$ inches in diameter.) Our imaginary sample, then, has a cross-section area of 1 square inch.

Tension

That pull (an engineer would call it a tension force) produces a stress in the material of the sample of 100 pounds per square inch—100 psi. If we pulled twice as hard, the stress would rise to 200 psi. If we doubled the size of the sample but kept the force at 100 pounds, the stress would drop to 50 psi. So, in this context, stress does not mean getting emotionally wound up because of family, money, job, or other troubles; it has a dead simple but specific mathematical definition:

$$S = \frac{P}{A}$$

where: S = stress, psi
P = load, lb
A = area, sq in

Compression

That same equation holds true if we push on (compress) the sample instead of pulling on it, but with one important condition attached—you have to be able to actually load the sample in compression. You cannot push on a

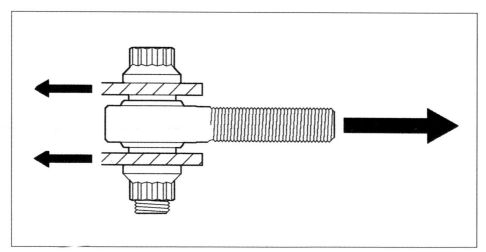

Figure 50: A force that tries to slice through things, such as this bolt's shank, produces a shear stress in the material.

rope; it just buckles out of the way! Likewise, a long slat of wood or a thin metal rod will also buckle. This issue of buckling is discussed below under "Columns." But if we cut a very short piece out of either, then we can in fact push on it until it crushes.

Shear

There is another way we can stress our imaginary piece of material—we can try to slice through, or *shear*, it (see figure 7-1). $S = \frac{P}{A}$ applies then, too. Suppose the bolt securing the balljoint rod end in figure 7-1 is $\frac{1}{2}$ inch in diameter. Its cross-section area will be:

$$A = \pi r^2$$

$$= \pi \times (0.25)^2$$

$$= \pi \times 0.0625$$

$$= 0.196 \text{ sq in}$$

Now, as shown in figure 7-1, the bolt is arranged in *double shear*, that is, the bolt has to be sliced through in *two* places, one on each side of the rod end. The cross-section area the force is working against, then, is $2 \times 0.196 = 0.392$ sq in. If the rod end is applying a force of 1,000 pounds, then the *shear stress* in the bolt will be:

$$S_{shear} = \frac{P}{A}$$

$$S_{shear} = \frac{1,000}{0.392}$$

$$= 2,551 \text{ psi}$$

Strain

If you pull on a rubber band, it quite obviously stretches. But if you pull on a crowbar, it seems completely "rigid"—there seems to be no stretch at all. Yet, Sir Henry Royce was right—that crowbar is in fact stretching just as if it were made out of rubber. The reason it seems rigid is because the stretch is so small it is undetectable by human senses. The only time we become aware of this stretching is when the tiny, fractional percentage of increase in length (which is all that actually occurs with real materials in the real world) applies to something that is extremely long to begin with, and the material is heavily loaded. Think of the steel cables that hold up an elevator. The jiggle you feel when the elevator stops results from the weight of the elevator bouncing on the cable, which is rhythmically springing and rebounding. (A "spring," in fact, is just a piece of material that is arranged so that a force applied to it acts, one way or another, over a great length of the material. Sir Henry was right: all solid materials behave like springs.)

This slight change in length under load is what engineers mean when they talk about *strain*. Specifically, strain is the change in length per unit of original length. Although the *idea* of strain may be hard to get your head around, the math is dead simple:

$$\varepsilon = \frac{l}{L}$$

where: ε = strain (no units)
l = change in length, or stretch (any units)
L = original length (same units as l)

We are going to have to postpone providing a worked example for $\varepsilon = \frac{l}{L}$ because, while we can assume any figure we want for L, at the moment we have no idea what l might be. So, we first have to look at *stiffness*.

Stiffness

Henry Royce's pronouncement came within living memory, but it seems the idea behind his statement was first grasped nearly 300 years ago, by Robert Hooke (a very weird dude indeed, by the way). By a combination of experiment and pure reasoning, Hooke also came up with an expression about the relationship between stress and strain: "*Ut tensio,*" he said (in Latin), "*sic uis*" (As stress, so strain). Ten generations later, this is one of the first things engineers are taught: strain is proportional to stress. Not only does every material behave like a spring, that spring has a linear rate. Pull with 100 pounds of force on a

---

Table 3
Approximate Values of "E" and "G" for Some Common Materials

	E, psi 10^6	G, psi 10^6
Cast iron	12–17	5–6.8
Steel	30	11.4
Aluminum	10.5	3.8
Magnesium	6.5	2.5
Titanium	15–16.5	6–6.5
Spruce wood	1.4	na
Rubber	0.001	na
Fiberglass/epoxy	7–8	na
Carbon fiber/epoxy	16	na

crowbar and it will stretch a certain amount; pull with 200 pounds of force and it will stretch twice as far, and so on.

A lifetime after Hooke, another very strange man named Thomas Young came up with another proposition that is likely the second thing that engineers are taught: everything is a spring, but some materials are stiffer springs than others. Make a crowbar out of aluminum, for example, and it will stretch a different amount for a given pull (more, as it turns out) than one made from steel. The way Young expressed it:

where: S = stress (any units)
ε = strain (no units)
E = a constant for any material (same units as for S)

E has become known as "Young's modulus," and is found in a great many engineering calculations, naturally including those involving springs (see, for example, "Leaf Springs" in chapter 4, Chassis Math). The values of E for some common engineering materials are listed in table 3.

So, now we can return to the task of trying to stretch a crowbar and learning why it seems "rigid." Let's suppose you eat your spinach and work out at the gym a lot, so you can pull on the opposite ends of a crowbar with a force of 100 pounds. Let's say the crowbar is made of steel, is 2 feet (24 inches) long and is $\frac{3}{4}$ inch in diameter.

The cross-section area will be:

$$A = \pi r^2$$

$$= \pi \left(\frac{0.75}{2} \right)^2$$

$$\cong 0.442 \text{ sq in}$$

So the stress will be:

$$S = \frac{P}{A}$$

$$= \frac{100}{0.442}$$

$$\cong 226 \text{ psi}$$

From these two, we can figure out the strain, as follows:

$$\frac{S}{\varepsilon} = E$$

$$\therefore \varepsilon = \frac{S}{E}$$

$$= \frac{226}{30,000,000}$$

$$\cong 0.0000075$$

The bar started off 24 inches long, so the strain will add $0.0000075 \times 24 = 0.00018$ inch—less than two ten-thousandths of an inch, which is a challenge to measure even with a Vernier micrometer—and that is why we think the crowbar is "rigid."

Strength

Stress, we have said, is the load applied to a piece of something per unit of area of that piece. The *strength* of a material (the stuff that the thing is made from) is simply the stress required to break it. For many common materials—wood, bricks, glass—that is all there is to it; the stuff acts like a spring, stretching in proportion to the applied force (and springing back when the load is removed) right up to the point where the stress exceeds the material's ability to resist, at which point it breaks. If the load acts so as to pull the material apart, that limit is called the *Ultimate Tensile Strength* (UTS, or S_{tu}). If the load tries to crush the material, that limit is the material's *Ultimate Compressive Strength* (UCS, or S_{cu}). And if the load acts so as to try to slice through (shear) the material, the limit is called the *Ultimate Shear Strength* (S_{su}—for some reason, USS is seldom, if ever, used). The values of S_{tu}, S_{cu}, and S_{su} for some common materials are listed in table 4.

Table 4

Typical Strengths of Some Common Materials, 103psi

	Sty/Stu	Scy/Scu	Ssy/Ssu
Cast iron	30-–50/30–50	100–175/100–175	45–75/45–75
1045 Steel	50–150/80–180	50–150/80–180	38–110/60–130
Wrought aluminum	40–50/60–80	40–50/60–80	20–30/30–50
Cast magnesium	15–25/25–40	15–25/25–40	12–20/15–20
Titanium	75–140/85–180	75–140/85–180	n.a./55–110
Spruce wood1	8–12/n.a	3–5/5–8	na
Rubber	na/1–3	na	na
Fiberglass/epoxy	50–90/50–90	40–70/40–70	na
Carbon fib/epoxy	75–150/75–150	50–120/50–120	3–8/3–8

note 1: measured parallel to grain

Let's suppose our crowbar is made from 1045 steel. Table 4 indicates that the UTS of this material is anywhere between 80,000 psi and 180,000 psi (depending on heat treatment, a subject well outside the scope of this book). Let's pick a high value of 170,000 psi. Recall that the crowbar has a cross-section area of 0.442 square inch. The load to rip it apart lengthwise, then, is simply 0.442 × 170,000 = 75,140 lb—more than 37 tons.

And just for fun, let's figure out how far the 24-inch-long bar would have stretched by the time it breaks.

$$\varepsilon = \frac{S}{E}$$

$$= \frac{75,140}{30,000,000}$$

$$\cong 0.0025 \text{ times the original length}$$

Based on the original length of 24 inches, the strain would total 0.0025 × 24 = 0.06 inch, so even when literally stretched to the breaking point, the stretch is minuscule.

Table 4 also lists values marked S_{ty}, S_{cy}, and S_{sy} for those same materials. These refer, respectively, to the tensile, compressive, and shear *yield* strengths, and this requires a bit of explanation. While many (indeed, most) common materials behave just as described above, one very important category of materials—common structural metals—show an interesting wrinkle. While they behave like springs for small to medium-sized loads, as the stress rises higher the material will continue to extend (or compress, or whatever), but some of the stretch will become permanent—the material will not fully spring back to its original size when the load is removed.

When metals are heat-treated to high strength levels, their UTS increases, but the yield strength generally increases even more, so the spread narrows between the point at which a permanent "set" becomes apparent and the point at which it goes bang. We deliberately picked a high value for the strength of the steel in the crowbar so the example would be vaguely realistic. If we had chosen, say, 80,000 psi, then that *yielding* would have set in long before the ultimate strength had been reached, so the actual measurable increase in length would have been much more than what we might calculate based on the reversible, "springy" part of the action.

Torsion

Much the same thing happens when materials are loaded in shear. We touched on this above, when figuring out the shear stress in a bolt securing a rod end. The situation described there was a very simple one—all the material in the bolt is equally stressed. Another way that materials get stressed in shear

Figure 51
A shear stress is also induced when a shaft is subject to torsion. At any imaginary plane crossing the length of the shaft, the material on each side of that plane is trying to slide past the adjacent material.

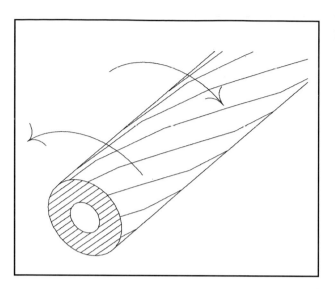

is when they are twisted. Consider a solid shaft with torque applied to it, and think about what is going on at any imaginary "slice" across that bar. Wherever we look, the material on one side of the "slice" is trying to slide past the material on the other side, in exactly the same way that the portion of the bolt that lies within the ball of the rod end in figure 50 is trying to slide past the bolt material immediately outboard of the ball.

But unlike the material in the bolt, the shear stress that arises when we twist something is *not* uniform across the section. As mentioned when considering torsion bars in chapter 4, Chassis Math, a hollow torsion bar saves weight because the material toward the center of a solid bar is only very lightly stressed, and is better replaced with considerably less material added near the outside surface. Think of it this way: For a given angle of twist, material near the outside surface has to stretch further (that is, *strain* more) than material closer to the middle (see figure 52).

The equation to calculate the maximum stress (that is, the stress at the outer surface) of a solid torsion bar, or any other solid circular shaft loaded in torsion is:

$$S_{s\,max} = \frac{2T}{\pi r^3}$$

where: $S_{s\,max}$ = maximum shear stress, psi
T = applied torque, in-lb
r = radius of the bar or shaft, inches

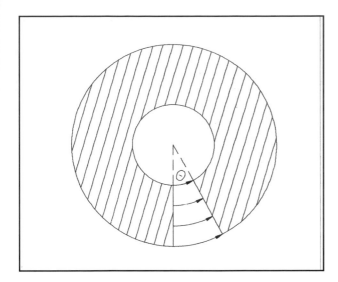

Figure 52
The shear stress is
highest at the outer
surface—because the
material there has to
move (strain) further.
The material in the
middle contributes next
to nothing, which is why
hollow torsion bars
make sense.

For example, consider a torsion bar with a *diameter* of 1.125 inches (or *radius* of 0.5625 inch) that has 4,800 in-lb (= 400 ft-lb) torque applied to it:

$$S_{s\,max} = \frac{2T}{\pi r^3}$$

$$= \frac{2 \times 4,800}{\pi(\,0.5625\,)^{\,3}}$$

$$\cong \frac{9,600}{\pi(\,0.178\,)}$$

$$\cong 17,169 \text{ psi}$$

This is well within the ultimate shear strength of any heat-treated alloy steel. Let's suppose that the S_{su} of the shaft material is 135,000 psi. We can then calculate the maximum torque the same shaft could withstand, as follows:

$$S_{s\,max} = \frac{2T}{\pi r^3} = 135,000$$

$$\frac{2T}{\pi r^3} = 135,000$$

$$2T = 135,000(\pi r^3)$$

(continued next page)

$$T = \frac{135,000(\pi r^3)}{2}$$

$$= \frac{135,000 \cdot \pi \cdot (0.5625)^{3}}{2}$$

$$\cong 37,742 \text{ in-lb}$$

If we want to calculate the angle of twist resulting from a torque applied to a solid shaft, the following equation can be used:

$$\theta = \frac{360Tl}{\pi^2 r^4 G}$$

where: θ = angle of twist, degrees
            T = applied torque, in-lb
            l = length of the shaft, inches
            r = radius of the shaft, inches
            G = torsional modulus of the shaft material, psi
(Table 3 also lists the value of G for the same materials.)

Consider the same bar as above, under the same 4,800 in-lb torque. Let's suppose it is 32 inches long:

$$\theta = \frac{360Tl}{\pi^2 r^4 G}$$

$$= \frac{360 \times 4,800 \times 32}{\pi^2 (0.5625^4)(11,500,000)}$$

$$\cong \frac{55,296,000}{\pi^2 (1,151,298)}$$

$$\cong 4.866 \text{ degrees}$$

For *hollow* circular bars and shafts, the maximum shear stress can be calculated with the following equation:

$$S_{s\,max} = \frac{2Tr_1}{\pi(r_1^4 - r_2^4)}$$

where: $S_{s\,max}$ = maximum shear stress, psi
            T = applied torque, in-lb
            r = the *outside* radius of the bar, inches
            r_2 = the *inside* radius of the bar, inches

Consider the same torsion bar as used in the previous example, with the same 4,800 in-lb torque applied to it, except this time we rifle-drill a $\frac{5}{8}$-inch hole down the center of the bar, so $r_2 = \frac{5}{16} = 0.3125$ inch:

$$S_{s\,max} = \frac{2Tr_1}{\pi(r_1^4 - r_2^4)}$$

$$= \frac{2 \times 4{,}800 \times 0.5625}{\pi(0.5625^4 - 0.3125^4)}$$

$$\cong \frac{2 \times 4{,}800 \times 0.5625}{\pi(0.100113 - 0.009537)}$$

$$\cong \frac{5{,}400}{\pi(0.090576)}$$

$$\cong 18{,}977 \text{ psi}$$

Note that even though we have eliminated more than 30 percent of the material (and so the weight) compared to the solid bar, the peak stress in the remaining material is only increased by about 10.5 percent.

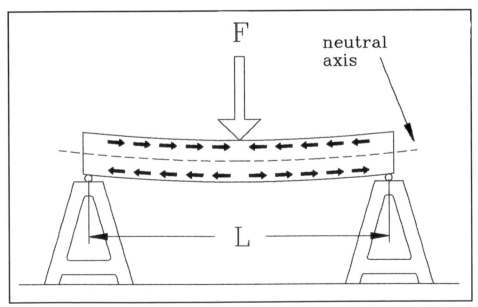

Figure 53: What appears to be a bending load actually turns out to be a combination of tension in one surface and compression in the other. Again, material in the middle—along the "neutral axis"—experiences no stress at all.

The equation for calculating the angle of twist of a hollow bar or shaft is:

$$\theta = \frac{360Tl}{\pi^2(r_1^4 - r_2^4)G}$$

where: θ = angle of twist, degrees
T = applied torque, in-lb
l = length of the shaft, inches
r_1 = the *outside* radius of the bar, inches
r_2 = the *inside* radius of the bar, inches
G = torsional modulus of the shaft material, psi

Let's again use the same bar as above, under the same torsional load as in the previous solid bar example:

$$\theta = \frac{360Tl}{\pi^2(r_1^4 - r_2^4)G}$$

$$= \frac{360 \times 4{,}800 \times 32}{\pi^2(0.5625^4 - 0.3125^4)(11{,}500{,}000)}$$

$$= \frac{55{,}296{,}000}{\pi^2(0.098697 - 0.009537)(11{,}500{,}000)}$$

$$\cong \frac{55{,}296{,}000}{\pi^2(1{,}041{,}626)}$$

$$\cong 5.379 \text{ degrees}$$

Beams and Bending

Generally speaking, just about anything that is supported at its ends and loaded in the middle is a beam. The chassis frame of an automobile is a familiar example: The weight of the engine, occupants, and all the other bits press down on the frame in the middle, while the support for all this weight is provided by the axles, which are roughly at the ends. Surely the great-grand-daddy of all beams is a tree, felled across a river, ravine, or other gap to serve as a bridge. (Indeed, the word *beam* is the Old English form of the word *tree*; in German, *Baum* still means tree.)

When we load a beam by applying a force in its middle, such as by standing on it, we tend to bend it. If the beam is thin enough in relation to the load and the span, we can see this bend quite distinctly. What is actually going on here is that the upper surface gets squeezed somewhat shorter, while the lower surface stretches somewhat; the curvature of the beam is just a result of this difference in length between top and bottom surfaces (see figure 53). A "bending" load, then, is not a distinctive, unique type of loading but is simply a matter of a single piece of material experiencing a compression load in some areas and a tension load in others.

Just as the material right at the surface of a bar or shaft in torsion "springs" more—is strained further—than material nearer the middle (see "Torsion," above), so the material right at the upper and lower surfaces of a beam is stretched or compressed further than is the stuff near the middle, and likewise is more highly stressed. And there is a line down the center of the beam—called the *neutral axis*—that experiences no tension or compression stress at all. The load a beam can carry without either tearing apart the material experiencing a tensile stress or crushing the material bearing a compressive stress is determined, then, by the stress at the surfaces.

For a simple beam of regular cross-section, as illustrated in figure 53, the maximum stress in the area of the top and bottom surfaces (any tiny part of which is sometimes called an *extreme fiber*) is given by:

$$S_{max} = \frac{M_{max}\,c}{I}$$

where: S_{max} = maximum tensile or compressive stress, psi
M_{max} = maximum bending moment, in-lb
c = distance of surface from neutral axis, inches
I = moment of inertia of the section, in^4

These terms need a little further explanation. M_{max} is the maximum *bending moment* acting on the beam. The units for M are units of length times units of force, i.e., in-lb or ft-lb (think torque). Referring to figure 54, in general:

$$M_{max} = \frac{Fab}{L}$$

If the load is applied in the exact middle of the beam, as in figure 53,

$$M_{max} = \frac{FL}{4}$$

For a beam whose cross-section is symmetrical about a horizontal plane (that is, the top and bottom are mirror images of each other), such as a square or rectangle or circle, c is simply half the depth of the beam.

The term I—the *moment of inertia* or *second moment of area* of the section—is a little trickier. These cumbersome and puzzling expressions refer to the combined effects of "how much stuff is there?" and "how far is 'there' from

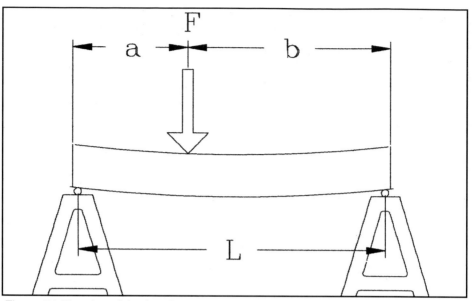

Figure 54: The size of the bending load in a beam depends on the size of the force and also on the position along the beam where that force is applied. If the force is applied at one extreme end, then there is no bending load at all; the maximum occurs when the force is applied in the middle.

the neutral axis?" If you have a selection of different sized round tubes, for example, each of which will just fit around the next smaller one, then as you "nest" each larger one around the existing stack, there is obviously more stuff in total. But you could also add material by sticking smaller tubes down the middle. The two situations are not the same because by adding larger tubes to the outside, all the added material lies further from the neutral axis, so the value of I will increase. Values for I for some common cross-sections are given in table 5.

For example, consider a simple beam, 6 inches square, and supported at two points 100 inches apart. Let's imagine it is loaded in the middle by a force of 2,000 pounds. M_{max}, then, is $\frac{2,000 \times 100}{4} = 50,000$ in-lb, while c is obviously 3 inches. From table 5, $I = 108$. So:

$$S_{max} = \frac{M_{max}\, c}{I}$$

$$= \frac{50,000 \times 3}{108}$$

$$\cong 1,389 \text{ psi}$$

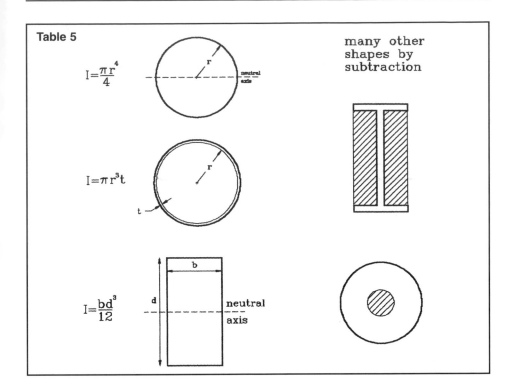

Table 5

$$I=\frac{\pi r^4}{4}$$

$$I=\pi r^3 t$$

$$I=\frac{bd^3}{12}$$

many other shapes by subtraction

As long as the maximum stress is less than either the compressive or tensile strength of the material the beam is made from, the beam will support the load without breaking.

Columns

If we apply a sufficiently large compressive load to something short and dumpy, like a brick, we will succeed in crushing it. If it is actually a brick, or any other squat-shaped object made of a brittle material like glass or cast iron, the result will be a bang and small heap of fragments. On the other hand, if the object is made from something that is capable of permanently deforming without breaking, like modeling clay or a fairly soft metal, the object will change shape, squeezing shorter and swelling in width. That is what happens when an engine bearing gets "pounded out."

But if an object loaded in compression is comparatively long and thin, like a pushrod, the effect of an overload will be to buckle the part, rather than to crush it. In practice, we would find that as we gradually increase the load, the pushrod (say) will sustain the load with no apparent grief up to some critical stress, then suddenly bow into a curve. Beyond that point, increasing the load will just cause the curvature to increase. In engineering terms, this is a *long column*, and a long column will fail by buckling at a load far, far below the compressive strength of the material it is made from. In fact, the load at failure does not depend on the *strength* of the material at all, but simply on the *stiffness* of the material and on the shape of the object—specifically its length-to-thickness ratio, or *slenderness*.

Mathematically:

$$F_{cr} = (c)\frac{\pi^2 EI}{L^2}$$

where: F_{cr} = critical buckling load, lb
E = Young's modulus, psi (see "Stiffness," above)
I = moment of inertia, inch⁴ (see "Beams and Bending")
L = length of column, inches
c = "end restraint factor" (see note below)

The "end restraint factor," c, in the above equation can have a value anywhere between 1 and 4, depending on the particular arrangement of things at the ends of the column. If both ends of the column are "pin-jointed," that is, free to rotate, then c has a value of 1; if both ends are completely prevented from swiveling, then c can be as large as 4. The idea here is that while a column

Figure 55
The resistance of a thin strut against buckling depends on how the ends are attached. If the "end fixity" is high (right), say by being part of a welded frame, the strut has to adopt a double-"S"-shape to deform at all. If the ends are "pin-jointed" (left), say through balljoint rod ends, it will spring into a simpler C-shaped curvature at a much lower load.

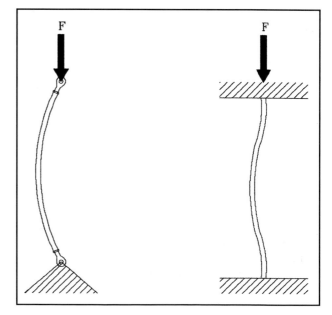

that is free to swivel at its ends will buckle into a simple "C" shape, one with solidly anchored ends has to adopt a double-"S"-shaped curve in order to buckle at all (see figure 55).

A simple suspension or steering link with a balljoint at either end is a common example of a "pin-jointed" column ($c = 1$). A single tube in a space frame, restricted from swiveling at the ends because it is welded to other tubes, will have end conditions that may come close to $c = 4$. But only close, because nothing is perfectly stiff, so while the other tubes will provide some resistance to swiveling, they will not be able to completely prevent it. Aircraft designers often use a conservative value of $c = 2$ in such circumstances.

Let's use as an example a suspension link that is 40 inches long and is made from $\frac{3}{4}$-inch chrome-moly (4130) steel tubing with a wall thickness of 0.035 inch.

$$F_{cr} = (c)\frac{\pi^2 EI}{L^2}$$

We assume that the link has a balljoint at each end, so $c = 1$. From table 3, $E = 30,000,000$. From table 5, for thin-walled tubes $I = \pi r^3 t$. Here, $r = 0.375$ and $t = 0.035$, so:

$$I = \pi r^3 t$$

$$= \pi(0.375)^3(0.035)$$

$$= \pi(0.0527)(0.035)$$

$$\cong 0.0058$$

Plugging all this into the above equation:

$$F_{cr} = 1 \times \frac{\pi^2(30,000,000)(0.0058)}{40^2}$$

$$\cong \frac{9.8696(30,000,000)(0.0058)}{40^2}$$

$$\cong 1,073 \text{ lb}$$

Let's compare this to the force required to actually crush, rather than buckle, a *short* section of the same chrome moly tubing. From table 4, the S_{cy} for this material is 60,000 psi. The cross-section area of a 0.75 × 0.035 tube is approximately 0.08 square inch, so the required force is simply $60,000 \times 0.08 = 4,800$ lb.

It is worth asking just how short the link would have to be in order to be crushed, rather than buckled. In other words, how do we know we are dealing with a "long column"? If the link were shorter, L^2 would be smaller, so the value of F_{cr} would be larger. At some point, the critical buckling load would equal the compressive yield strength of the material.

$$F_{cr} = (c)\frac{\pi^2 EI}{L^2} = S_{cy}$$

We have assumed $c = 1$, so:

$$\frac{\pi^2 EI}{L^2} = 60{,}000$$

$$60{,}000L^2 = \pi^2 EI$$

$$L^2 = \frac{\pi^2(30{,}000{,}000)(0.0058)}{60{,}000}$$

$$\cong 28.62$$

$$\therefore\ L \cong \sqrt{28.62}$$

$$\cong 5.34 \text{ inches}$$

In automobiles, aircraft, and anything else that moves under its own power, weight is important. Accordingly, engineers try to arrange for things like pushrods and suspension links and space frames to be as light as possible while still retaining adequate strength and stiffness.

Because the value of I, and so the value of F_{cr}, increases as the *cube* of the radius of a tube, while the amount of material only increases linearly, a very considerable weight saving results from increasing the tube diameter and reducing its wall thickness. There is a limit to how far this can be carried, however. Eventually you get to the point where a small area of the tube wall will crumple before the critical buckling load for the column as a whole is reached. This is what happens when you step squarely on the end of a beer can. For each material, there is some critical ratio of diameter to wall thickness above which the wall will suffer this *local crippling*, as it is called.

Although this critical ratio can, in theory, be calculated mathematically, the fact is that none of the various published equations correspond very well with real world experience. What can be said is that for steel tubing, a long column will buckle before the walls wrinkle as long as the diameter is less than 50 times the wall thickness. Notably, the sizes of steel tubing certified for aircraft construction generally exclude diameter/wall thickness ratios that exceed about 32:1.

Appendix

Trigonometry Table

angle	sin	cosine	tangent	cotan
0	0	1	0	undefined
1	0.017452	0.999848	0.017455	57.298688
2	0.034899	0.999391	0.034921	28.653708
3	0.052336	0.998630	0.052408	19.107323
4	0.069756	0.997564	0.069927	14.335587
5	0.087156	0.996195	0.087489	11.473713
6	0.104528	0.994522	0.105104	9.566772
7	0.121869	0.992546	0.122785	8.205509
8	0.139173	0.990268	0.140541	7.185297
9	0.156434	0.987688	0.158384	6.392453
10	0.173648	0.984808	0.176327	5.758770
11	0.190809	0.981627	0.194380	5.240843
12	0.207912	0.978148	0.212557	4.809734
13	0.224951	0.974370	0.230868	4.445411
14	0.241922	0.970296	0.249328	4.133565
15	0.258819	0.965926	0.267949	3.863703
16	0.275637	0.961262	0.286745	3.627955
17	0.292372	0.956305	0.305731	3.420304
18	0.309017	0.951057	0.324920	3.236068
19	0.325568	0.945519	0.344328	3.071553
20	0.342020	0.939693	0.363970	2.923804
21	0.358368	0.933580	0.383864	2.790428
22	0.374607	0.927184	0.404026	2.669467
23	0.390731	0.920505	0.424475	2.559305
24	0.406737	0.913545	0.445229	2.458593
25	0.422618	0.906308	0.466308	2.366202
26	0.438371	0.898794	0.487733	2.281172
27	0.453990	0.891007	0.509525	2.202689
28	0.469472	0.882948	0.531709	2.130054
29	0.484810	0.874620	0.554309	2.062665
30	0.500000	0.866025	0.577350	2.000000
31	0.515038	0.857167	0.600861	1.941604
32	0.529919	0.848048	0.624869	1.887080
33	0.544639	0.838671	0.649408	1.836078
34	0.559193	0.829038	0.674509	1.788292
35	0.573576	0.819152	0.700208	1.743447
36	0.587785	0.809017	0.726543	1.701302
37	0.601815	0.798636	0.753554	1.661640
38	0.615661	0.788011	0.781286	1.624269
39	0.629320	0.777146	0.809784	1.589016
40	0.642788	0.766044	0.839100	1.555724
41	0.656059	0.754710	0.869287	1.524253
42	0.669131	0.743145	0.900404	1.494477
43	0.681998	0.731354	0.932515	1.466229
44	0.694658	0.719340	0.965689	1.439557
45	0.707107	0.707107	1.000000	1.414214
46	0.719340	0.694658	1.035530	1.390164
47	0.731354	0.681998	1.072369	1.367327
48	0.743145	0.669131	1.110613	1.345633
49	0.754710	0.656059	1.150368	1.325013
50	0.766044	0.642788	1.191754	1.305407
51	0.777146	0.629320	1.234897	1.286760
52	0.788011	0.615661	1.279942	1.269018
53	0.798636	0.601815	1.327045	1.252136
54	0.809017	0.587785	1.376382	1.236068

angle	sin	cosine	tangent	cotan
55	0.819152	0.573576	1.428148	1.220775
56	0.829038	0.559193	1.482561	1.206218
57	0.838671	0.544639	1.539865	1.192363
58	0.848048	0.529919	1.600335	1.179178
59	0.857167	0.515038	1.664279	1.166633
60	0.866025	0.500000	1.732051	1.154701
61	0.874620	0.484810	1.804048	1.143354
62	0.882948	0.469472	1.880726	1.132570
63	0.891007	0.453990	1.962611	1.122326
64	0.898794	0.438371	2.050304	1.112602
65	0.906308	0.422618	2.144507	1.103378
66	0.913545	0.406737	2.246037	1.094636
67	0.920505	0.390731	2.355852	1.086360
68	0.927184	0.374607	2.475087	1.078535
69	0.933580	0.358368	2.605089	1.071145
70	0.939693	0.342020	2.747477	1.064178
71	0.945519	0.325568	2.904211	1.057621
72	0.951057	0.309017	3.077684	1.051462
73	0.956305	0.292372	3.270853	1.045692
74	0.961262	0.275637	3.487414	1.040299
75	0.965926	0.258819	3.732051	1.035276
76	0.970296	0.241922	4.010781	1.030614
77	0.974370	0.224951	4.331476	1.026304
78	0.978148	0.207912	4.704630	1.022341
79	0.981627	0.190809	5.144554	1.018717
80	0.984808	0.173648	5.671282	1.015427
81	0.987688	0.156434	6.313752	1.012465
82	0.990268	0.139173	7.115370	1.009828
83	0.992546	0.121869	8.144346	1.007510
84	0.994522	0.104528	9.514364	1.005508
85	0.996195	0.087156	11.430052	1.003820
86	0.997564	0.069756	14.300666	1.002442
87	0.998630	0.052336	19.081137	1.001372
88	0.999391	0.034899	28.636253	1.000610
89	0.999848	0.017452	57.289962	1.000152
90	1.000000	0.000000	undefined.	1.000000
91	0.999848	-0.017452	-57.289962	1.000152
92	0.999391	-0.034899	-28.636253	1.000610
93	0.998630	-0.052336	-19.081137	1.001372
94	0.997564	-0.069756	-14.300666	1.002442
95	0.996195	-0.087156	-11.430052	1.003820
96	0.994522	-0.104528	-9.514364	1.005508
97	0.992546	-0.121869	-8.144346	1.007510
98	0.990268	-0.139173	-7.115370	1.009828
99	0.987688	-0.156434	-6.313752	1.012465
100	0.984808	-0.173648	-5.671282	1.015427
101	0.981627	-0.190809	-5.144554	1.018717
102	0.978148	-0.207912	-4.704630	1.022341
103	0.974370	-0.224951	-4.331476	1.026304
104	0.970296	-0.241922	-4.010781	1.030614
105	0.965926	-0.258819	-3.732051	1.035276
106	0.961262	-0.275637	-3.487414	1.040299
107	0.956305	-0.292372	-3.270853	1.045692
108	0.951057	-0.309017	-3.077684	1.051462
109	0.945519	-0.325568	-2.904211	1.057621
110	0.939693	-0.342020	-2.747477	1.064178
111	0.933580	-0.358368	-2.605089	1.071145
112	0.927184	-0.374607	-2.475087	1.078535
113	0.920505	-0.390731	-2.355852	1.086360
114	0.913545	-0.406737	-2.246037	1.094636
115	0.906308	-0.422618	-2.144507	1.103378
116	0.898794	-0.438371	-2.050304	1.112602

angle	sin	cosine	tangent	cotan
117	0.891007	-0.453990	-1.962611	1.122326
118	0.882948	-0.469472	-1.880726	1.132570
119	0.874620	-0.484810	-1.804048	1.143354
120	0.866025	-0.500000	-1.732051	1.154701
121	0.857167	-0.515038	-1.664279	1.166633
122	0.848048	-0.529919	-1.600335	1.179178
123	0.838671	-0.544639	-1.539865	1.192363
124	0.829038	-0.559193	-1.482561	1.206218
125	0.819152	-0.573576	-1.428148	1.220775
126	0.809017	-0.587785	-1.376382	1.236068
127	0.798636	-0.601815	-1.327045	1.252136
128	0.788011	-0.615661	-1.279942	1.269018
129	0.777146	-0.629320	-1.234897	1.286760
130	0.766044	-0.642788	-1.191754	1.305407
131	0.754710	-0.656059	-1.150368	1.325013
132	0.743145	-0.669131	-1.110613	1.345633
133	0.731354	-0.681998	-1.072369	1.367327
134	0.719340	-0.694658	-1.035530	1.390164
135	0.707107	-0.707107	-1.000000	1.414214
136	0.694658	-0.719340	-0.965689	1.439557
137	0.681998	-0.731354	-0.932515	1.466279
138	0.669131	-0.743145	-0.900404	1.494477
139	0.656059	-0.754710	-0.869287	1.524253
140	0.642788	-0.766044	-0.839100	1.555724
141	0.629320	-0.777146	-0.809784	1.589016
142	0.615661	-0.788011	-0.781286	1.624269
143	0.601815	-0.798636	-0.753554	1.661640
144	0.587785	-0.809017	-0.726543	1.701302
145	0.573576	-0.819152	-0.700208	1.743447
146	0.559193	-0.829038	-0.674509	1.788292
147	0.544639	-0.838671	-0.649408	1.836078
148	0.529919	-0.848048	-0.624869	1.887080
149	0.515038	-0.857167	-0.600861	1.941604
150	0.500000	-0.866025	-0.577350	2.000000
151	0.484810	-0.874620	-0.554309	2.062665
152	0.469472	-0.882948	-0.531709	2.130054
153	0.453990	-0.891007	-0.509525	2.202689
154	0.438371	-0.898794	-0.487733	2.281172
155	0.422618	-0.906308	-0.466308	2.366202
156	0.406737	-0.913545	-0.445229	2.458593
157	0.390731	-0.920505	-0.424475	2.559305
158	0.374607	-0.927184	-0.404026	2.669467
159	0.358368	-0.933580	-0.383864	2.790428
160	0.342020	-0.939693	-0.363970	2.923804
161	0.325568	-0.945519	-0.344328	3.071553
162	0.309017	-0.951057	-0.324920	3.236068
163	0.292372	-0.956305	-0.305731	3.420304
164	0.275637	-0.961262	-0.286745	3.627955
165	0.258819	-0.965926	-0.267949	3.863703
166	0.241922	-0.970296	-0.249328	4.133565
167	0.224951	-0.974370	-0.230868	4.445411
168	0.207912	-0.978148	-0.212557	4.809734
169	0.190809	-0.981627	-0.194380	5.240843
170	0.173648	-0.984808	-0.176327	5.758770
171	0.156434	-0.987688	-0.158384	6.392453
172	0.139173	-0.990268	-0.140541	7.185297
173	0.121869	-0.992546	-0.122785	8.205509
174	0.104528	-0.994522	-0.105104	9.566772
175	0.087156	-0.996195	-0.087489	11.473713
176	0.069756	-0.997564	-0.069927	14.335587
177	0.052336	-0.998630	-0.052408	19.107323
178	0.034899	-0.999391	-0.034921	28.653708

angle	sin	cosine	tangent	cotan
179	0.017452	-0.999848	-0.017455	57.298688
180	0.000000	-1.000000	0.000000	undefined
181	-0.017452	-0.999848	0.017455	-57.298688
182	-0.034899	-0.999391	0.034921	-28.653708
183	-0.052336	-0.998630	0.052408	-19.107323
184	-0.069756	-0.997564	0.069927	-14.335587
185	-0.087156	-0.996195	0.087489	-11.473713
186	-0.104528	-0.994522	0.105104	-9.566772
187	-0.121869	-0.992546	0.122785	-8.205509
188	-0.139173	-0.990268	0.140541	-7.185297
189	-0.156434	-0.987688	0.158384	-6.392453
190	-0.173648	-0.984808	0.176327	-5.758770
191	-0.190809	-0.981627	0.194380	-5.240843
192	-0.207912	-0.978148	0.212557	-4.809734
193	-0.224951	-0.974370	0.230868	-4.445411
194	-0.241922	-0.970296	0.249328	-4.133565
195	-0.258819	-0.965926	0.267949	-3.863703
196	-0.275637	-0.961262	0.286745	-3.627955
197	-0.292372	-0.956305	0.305731	-3.420304
198	-0.309017	-0.951057	0.324920	-3.236068
199	-0.325568	-0.945519	0.344328	-3.071553
200	-0.342020	-0.939693	0.363970	-2.923804
201	-0.358368	-0.933580	0.383864	-2.790428
202	-0.374607	-0.927184	0.404026	-2.669467
203	-0.390731	-0.920505	0.424475	-2.559305
204	-0.406737	-0.913545	0.445229	-2.458593
205	-0.422618	-0.906308	0.466308	-2.366202
206	-0.438371	-0.898794	0.487733	-2.281172
207	-0.453990	-0.891007	0.509525	-2.202689
208	-0.469472	-0.882948	0.531709	-2.130054
209	-0.484810	-0.874620	0.554309	-2.062665
210	-0.500000	-0.866025	0.577350	-2.000000
211	-0.515038	-0.857167	0.600861	-1.941604
212	-0.529919	-0.848048	0.624869	-1.887080
213	-0.544639	-0.838671	0.649408	-1.836078
214	-0.559193	-0.829038	0.674509	-1.788292
215	-0.573576	-0.819152	0.700208	-1.743447
216	-0.587785	-0.809017	0.726543	-1.701302
217	-0.601815	-0.798636	0.753554	-1.661640
218	-0.615661	-0.788011	0.781286	-1.624269
219	-0.629320	-0.777146	0.809784	-1.589016
220	-0.642788	-0.766044	0.839100	-1.555724
221	-0.656059	-0.754710	0.869287	-1.524253
222	-0.669131	-0.743145	0.900404	-1.494477
223	-0.681998	-0.731354	0.932515	-1.466279
224	-0.694658	-0.719340	0.965689	-1.439557
225	-0.707107	-0.707107	1.000000	-1.414214
226	-0.719340	-0.694658	1.035530	-1.390164
227	-0.731354	-0.681998	1.072369	-1.367327
228	-0.743145	-0.669131	1.110613	-1.345633
229	-0.754710	-0.656059	1.150368	-1.325013
230	-0.766044	-0.642788	1.191754	-1.305407
231	-0.777146	-0.629320	1.234897	-1.286760
232	-0.788011	-0.615661	1.279942	-1.269018
233	-0.798636	-0.601815	1.327045	-1.252136
234	-0.809017	-0.587785	1.376382	-1.236068
235	-0.819152	-0.573576	1.428148	-1.220775
236	-0.829038	-0.559193	1.482561	-1.206218
237	-0.838671	-0.544639	1.539865	-1.192363
238	-0.848048	-0.529919	1.600335	-1.179178
239	-0.857167	-0.515038	1.664279	-1.166633
240	-0.866025	-0.500000	1.732051	-1.154701

angle	sin	cosine	tangent	cotan
241	-0.874620	-0.484810	1.804048	-1.143354
242	-0.882948	-0.469472	1.880726	-1.132570
243	-0.891007	-0.453990	1.962611	-1.122326
244	-0.898794	-0.438371	2.050304	-1.112602
245	-0.906308	-0.422618	2.144507	-1.103378
246	-0.913545	-0.406737	2.246037	-1.094636
247	-0.920505	-0.390731	2.355852	-1.086360
248	-0.927184	-0.374607	2.475087	-1.078535
249	-0.933580	-0.358368	2.605089	-1.071145
250	-0.939693	-0.342020	2.747477	-1.064178
251	-0.945519	-0.325568	2.904211	-1.057621
252	-0.951057	-0.309017	3.077684	-1.051462
253	-0.956305	-0.292372	3.270853	-1.045692
254	-0.961262	-0.275637	3.487414	-1.040299
255	-0.965926	-0.258819	3.732051	-1.035276
256	-0.970296	-0.241922	4.010781	-1.030614
257	-0.974370	-0.224951	4.331476	-1.026304
258	-0.978148	-0.207912	4.704630	-1.022341
259	-0.981627	-0.190809	5.144554	-1.018717
260	-0.984808	-0.173648	5.671282	-1.015427
261	-0.987688	-0.156434	6.313752	-1.012465
262	-0.990268	-0.139173	7.115370	-1.009828
263	-0.992546	-0.121869	8.144346	-1.007510
264	-0.994522	-0.104528	9.514364	-1.005508
265	-0.996195	-0.087156	11.430052	-1.003820
266	-0.997564	-0.069756	14.300666	-1.002442
267	-0.998630	-0.052336	19.081137	-1.001372
268	-0.999391	-0.034899	28.636253	-1.000610
269	-0.999848	-0.017452	57.289962	-1.000152
270	-1.000000	0.000000	undefined.	-1.000000
271	-0.999848	0.017452	-57.289962	-1.000152
272	-0.999391	0.034899	-28.636253	-1.000610
273	-0.998630	0.052336	-19.081137	-1.001372
274	-0.997564	0.069756	-14.300666	-1.002442
275	-0.996195	0.087156	-11.430052	-1.003820
276	-0.994522	0.104528	-9.514364	-1.005508
277	-0.992546	0.121869	-8.144346	-1.007510
278	-0.990268	0.139173	-7.115370	-1.009828
279	-0.987688	0.156434	-6.313752	-1.012465
280	-0.984808	0.173648	-5.671282	-1.015427
281	-0.981627	0.190809	-5.144554	-1.018717
282	-0.978148	0.207912	-4.704630	-1.022341
283	-0.974370	0.224951	-4.331476	-1.026304
284	-0.970296	0.241922	-4.010781	-1.030614
285	-0.965926	0.258819	-3.732051	-1.035276
286	-0.961262	0.275637	-3.487414	-1.040299
287	-0.956305	0.292372	-3.270853	-1.045692
288	-0.951057	0.309017	-3.077684	-1.051462
289	-0.945519	0.325568	-2.904211	-1.057621
290	-0.939693	0.342020	-2.747477	-1.064178
291	-0.933580	0.358368	-2.605089	-1.071145
292	-0.927184	0.374607	-2.475087	-1.078535
293	-0.920505	0.390731	-2.355852	-1.086360
294	-0.913545	0.406737	-2.246037	-1.094636
295	-0.906308	0.422618	-2.144507	-1.103378
296	-0.898794	0.438371	-2.050304	-1.112602
297	-0.891007	0.453990	-1.962611	-1.122326
298	-0.882948	0.469472	-1.880726	-1.132570
299	-0.874620	0.484810	-1.804048	-1.143354
300	-0.866025	0.500000	-1.732051	-1.154701
301	-0.857167	0.515038	-1.664279	-1.166633
302	-0.848048	0.529919	-1.600335	-1.179178

angle	sin	cosine	tangent	cotan
303	-0.838671	0.544639	-1.539865	-1.192363
304	-0.829038	0.559193	-1.482561	-1.206218
305	-0.819152	0.573576	-1.428148	-1.220775
306	-0.809017	0.587785	-1.376382	-1.236068
307	-0.798636	0.601815	-1.327045	-1.252136
308	-0.788011	0.615661	-1.279942	-1.269018
309	-0.777146	0.629320	-1.234897	-1.286760
310	-0.766044	0.642788	-1.191754	-1.305407
311	-0.754710	0.656059	-1.150368	-1.325013
312	-0.743145	0.669131	-1.110613	-1.345633
313	-0.731354	0.681998	-1.072369	-1.367327
314	-0.719340	0.694658	-1.035530	-1.390164
315	-0.707107	0.707107	-1.000000	-1.414214
316	-0.694658	0.719340	-0.965689	-1.439557
317	-0.681998	0.731354	-0.932515	-1.466279
318	-0.669131	0.743145	-0.900404	-1.494477
319	-0.656059	0.754710	-0.869287	-1.524253
320	-0.642788	0.766044	-0.839100	-1.555724
321	-0.629320	0.777146	-0.809784	-1.589016
322	-0.615661	0.788011	-0.781286	-1.624269
323	-0.601815	0.798636	-0.753554	-1.661640
324	-0.587785	0.809017	-0.726543	-1.701302
325	-0.573576	0.819152	-0.700208	-1.743447
326	-0.559193	0.829038	-0.674509	-1.788292
327	-0.544639	0.838671	-0.649408	-1.836078
328	-0.529919	0.848048	-0.624869	-1.887080
329	-0.515038	0.857167	-0.600861	-1.941604
330	-0.500000	0.866025	-0.577350	-2.000000
331	-0.484810	0.874620	-0.554309	-2.062665
332	-0.469472	0.882948	-0.531709	-2.130054
333	-0.453990	0.891007	-0.509525	-2.202689
334	-0.438371	0.898794	-0.487733	-2.281172
335	-0.422618	0.906308	-0.466308	-2.366202
336	-0.406737	0.913545	-0.445229	-2.458593
337	-0.390731	0.920505	-0.424475	-2.559305
338	-0.374607	0.927184	-0.404026	-2.669467
339	-0.358368	0.933580	-0.383864	-2.790428
340	-0.342020	0.939693	-0.363970	-2.923804
341	-0.325568	0.945519	-0.344328	-3.071553
342	-0.309017	0.951057	-0.324920	-3.236068
343	-0.292372	0.956305	-0.305731	-3.420304
344	-0.275637	0.961262	-0.286745	-3.627955
345	-0.258819	0.965926	-0.267949	-3.863703
346	-0.241922	0.970296	-0.249328	-4.133565
347	-0.224951	0.974370	-0.230868	-4.445411
348	-0.207912	0.978148	-0.212557	-4.809734
349	-0.190809	0.981627	-0.194380	-5.240843
350	-0.173648	0.984808	-0.176327	-5.758770
351	-0.156434	0.987688	-0.158384	-6.392453
352	-0.139173	0.990268	-0.140541	-7.185297
353	-0.121869	0.992546	-0.122785	-8.205509
354	-0.104528	0.994522	-0.105104	-9.566772
355	-0.087156	0.996195	-0.087489	-11.473713
356	-0.069756	0.997564	-0.069927	-14.335587
357	-0.052336	0.998630	-0.052408	-19.107323
358	-0.034899	0.999391	-0.034921	-28.653708
359	-0.017452	0.999848	-0.017455	-57.298688
360	0.000000	1.000000	0.000000	undefined

Index